Raised Bed Gardening

Easily Build a Sustainable Organic Garden
With Less Space

Janet Wilson

Copyright © 2020 by Janet Wilson

ALL RIGHTS RESERVED

No part of this book may be reproduced, stored in a retrieval system, or transmitted in any form or by any means, electronic, mechanical, photocopying, recording, scanning, or otherwise, without the prior written permission of the publisher.

Limit of Liability/Disclaimer of Warranty: the publisher and the author make no representations or warranties with respect to the accuracy or completeness of the contents of this work and specifically disclaim all warranties, including without limitation warranties of fitness for a particular purpose. No warranty may be created or extended by sales or promotional materials. The advice and strategies contained herein may not be suitable for every situation. This work is sold with the understanding that the publisher is not engaged in rendering medical, legal or other professional advice or services. If professional assistance is required, the services of a competent professional person should be sought. Neither the publisher nor the author shall be liable for damages arising herefrom. The fact that an individual, organization or website is referred to in this work as a citation and/or potential source of further information does not mean that the author or the publisher endorses the information the individuals, organization or website may provide or recommendations they/it may make. Further, readers should be aware that websites listed on this work may have changed or disappeared between when this work was written and when it is read.
ISBN: 978-1-951791-49-0

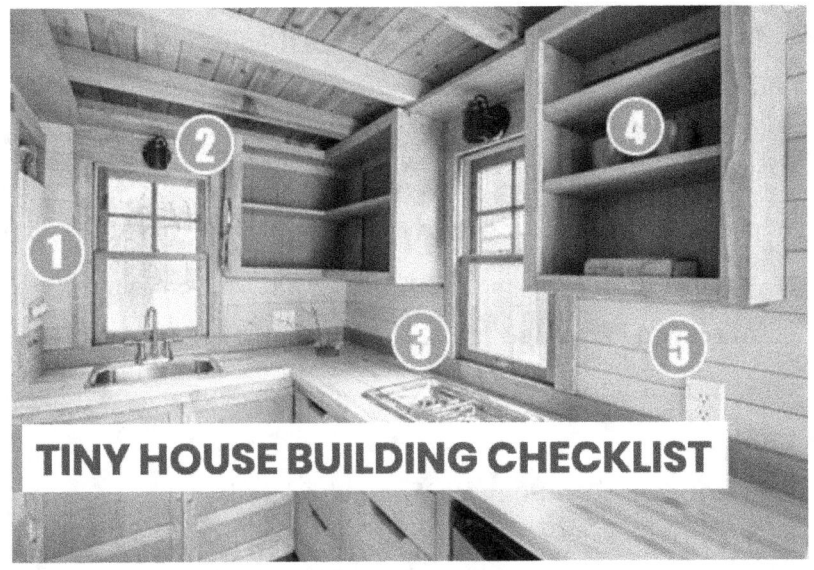

Get Your Free Checklist:

- Learn How To Build Your Own Tiny House
- Includes Tiny House Plans
- Access to a Private Sustainable Living Community

Visit:
Janetwilson.org

Table of Contents

Introduction 5
   Why Should I Grow a Garden? 6
   What are Raised Beds and Why Would I Want Them? 10

Part One: Set up Your Raised Beds 15
   Location and Planning 16
   Choose Your Raised Beds 23
   Location 59
   Accessories and Add-ons for Your Raised Beds 90
   Fencing 102

Part Two: Create Perfect Soil 116
   Creating the Perfect Soil 117
   Lasagna Composting for Raised Beds 119
   A Math Lesson 125

Part Three: Choose Your Plants and Maintain Your Garden 130
   Choosing the Right Plants 131
   Choosing Your Seeds 145
   Plant Your Seedlings 151
   Maintaining and Troubleshooting Your Garden 155

Conclusion 168

Introduction

Why Should I Grow a Garden?

Perhaps you've recently been thinking about growing a garden, but you don't have a clue where to begin?

If you are like many people, you don't know anything about soil types, and you only know that when you've tried to grow anything in your clay, it has died. If you live in the rocky mountain region of the western US, you know that you can't even plant a small herb without hitting a rock that you may not be able to move.

Some people don't think they can have a garden because they have a bad back, are in a wheelchair, or have other mobility challenges that make bending over and weeding a challenge. Some people hate the time it takes to weed and care for a garden. It isn't easy when you have children, a career, and a life outside of the home most of the time. Gardening is very time-consuming for many people.

How do you know what a weed is compared to vegetables that are growing? Where do you learn how to garden? Is it merely a waste of your time when you don't know where to begin? These are questions that run through the mind of many people who weren't raised in a family that had their own garden. In fact, there are more people alive right now who have never had a garden than at any other time in history.

Not only have we forgotten our roots -- no pun intended -- but we've become so dependent on a system that gets our foods to us, at a supermarket, where we get to pick the things that look the best. We've lost touch with the creative process by which healthy food is grown, we have become less healthy by eating foods that are not at their optimum peak of freshness.

In fact, more produce is picked weeks before it is ripe. If it were not picked very early, it would rot while being transported to stores. Instead, the farmers will pick crops just before their peak ripeness, and it will ripen in boxes and crates so that by the time it is getting to you, it very well is past its prime and turning brown. How many times do you see bananas at the store that are either green or brown? It's very difficult to find bananas that are perfectly ripe.

The largest portion of fruit available for sale in America now is actually imported from other countries. Not only does this mean that you are not eating 'fresh' fruits, it means that you don't know where they were grown exactly. Okay, maybe you know the country of origin, but you don't know what field and what contaminants are in that soil. These plants are called *phytoremediators*. *Phyto* means 'plant' and *remediation* means to remedy something.

Some foods are in a category of soil remediators. What this means is that they have high water content and are known for sucking everything up from the soil around them. Hemp is a very popular soil remediator. It is often planted in contaminated soils to clean heavy metals and other contaminants from that soil. This makes it viable for other things in the future.

That hemp, in the US, is then used for textiles, not for food or for ingesting in CBD products. Those that are imported, however, may have toxins present because they are not inspected, nor are they subject to the strict guidelines of our USDA (US Department of Agriculture). There are many vegetables that fall into this remediation group.

- Watercress
- Radish
- Turnips
- Cabbage
- Hemp (seeds)

There are other types of plants, but these are the top ones of which to be concerned. If you are eating produce that has been grown in another country, it could have been grown in contaminated soil, and you'd never even know. This is one truly good reason to eat foods grown in this country and definitely a case for growing your own food.

Eating locally grown produce has many benefits. Food from your garden, grown organically, will have a more robust flavor than those picked prior to ripening. Any food that is left to ripen on the vine will be bursting with flavor.

When you grow organically, you'll know that your food is safe to eat and you'll have the benefit of eating foods that are in season, which is wonderful for your body. Eating home-grown fruits and vegetables will help make you healthier, starting on the inside, at a cellular level.

Doing your own gardening is also a wonderful way to get your sunshine. Not all gardens require hours and hours of your time, but they will all require a little bit of your time, and when you are outdoors, enjoying the sunshine, your body will be soaking in the sunshine to help process Vitamin D.

Your lungs will be benefiting from the fresh oxygen that the plants are supplying to you as well. The plants will, in turn, be enjoying the carbon dioxide that you exhale. Plants and humans are a fine example of a symbiotic relationship.

So, now you understand why you should garden, yet you are still convinced that you cannot do it. What if you knew that there was a way to grow a garden that allowed for accessibility, was weed-free, and the soil was guaranteed to be perfectly suited to growing all sorts of fresh food? You'd jump right on that, wouldn't you?

Now you can. The intent is to introduce you to raised bed gardening that even a gardening beginner can handle. It doesn't have to be hard; in fact, we'll teach you how easy it can be and explain it all step by step so that anyone can understand and follow along. Let's get started.

What are Raised Beds and Why Would I Want Them?

In the most general of terms, a raised bed garden is any garden that is separated above the ground. It can be a box or container in any shape. It may be sitting directly on top of the ground as a weed barrier for the bottom, or it could be any container that is elevated to a height that is comfortable for you to access without bending or stooping.

Raised bed gardens are perfect for anyone (saves the back and the knees), but especially for those who have limitations on their mobility. If you've got the need to use a walker or a cane, your beds can be separated by enough distance to allow you to move between them and all the way around them. For every gardener of any age, they are easier on the body.

A pathway can be made around your beds, and you can use any material for your pathway that you'd like. You can incorporate gravel, woodchips, weed barrier on top of the ground, wood walkways, cement sidewalks, and even just cardboard on top of the ground to prevent weeds. You can make your garden accessible to you.

Raised bed gardens are predominantly weed-free, provided that you use soil that has been composted at a heat that was enough to destroy the weed seeds that were in it and that you keep your beds covered in off seasons so that weed seeds cannot blow into your beds and get started.

When you spot a weed in your raised bed, pull it and dispose of it so that it cannot go to seed in your bed. Weeding a raised bed garden doesn't have to be done much. You'll get the rare errant weed that managed to get seeded there by a bird or the wind.

The beauty in this is that anyone, with very little time or physical limitations, is capable of handling a raised bed garden. The hardest part is getting it set up to begin with. Once in place, your beds are good for years and don't really require a ton of work to prepare each year.

A raised bed can be built from scratch, purchased in a kit, or simply something you've repurposed for the cause. Everything from kiddie wading pools to old bathtubs is perfect in the raised bed gardening methods. This means that you can take the time and money to build something that looks beautiful and suits your style.

It also means you can grab an old canoe, drill some drain holes to go with the leak it had, and repurpose it into a raised bed garden. You can leave it to rest on the ground, or you can lift it up onto cement blocks, build a frame that is elaborate and beautiful or rest it atop an old spool from the utility company. Whatever *floats your boat* as they say.

One of the best attributes of the raised bed garden is that it is a blank slate for you to prep and plant however you'd like, and this is the strong appeal that it has for many people. It's simply what you need, where you need it.

Even if all you have is a back patio, one raised bed can grow a large amount of food for the apartment dwellers out there who have been seeking a way to have a garden. Strategically placed beds that are stacked over each other like a staircase can give you an enormous amount of room to grow food, allowing for expansion into the vast amount of 'up' that you have.

This might make you feel as if it is vertical gardening or container gardening. Yes, it can be a hybrid of all styles. Gardens are limited only to your creativity, space, and materials. Combining methods may prove to be what works best for you and your area. If it is right for you, then no one can tell you that it's wrong.

Here is an aerial view of an expansive raised bed garden. The designers thought about how to use the space and how to use centerpieces and levels to create interest.

This, of course, is in regard to the design and functionality of your garden. How it works and for which plants are more right or wrong; however, some people manage to adapt styles, soil types, and weather conditions to grow even difficult items by being a bit creative in how they grow their garden and care for it.

The one thing that is a given: once you try raised bed gardening, you'll likely never want to go back to any other way of planting. It's as close to a 'set it and forget it' type of garden that you can plant. There are so many variations that it can be highly individualized to fit your climate and needs.

The ultimate prize is heading outside to pick your fresh produce and taking it inside and creating a salad or a side dish for your meals that day, knowing that it was home-grown goodness you can depend on to be healthy and packed with nutrients.

Part One:
Set up Your Raised Beds

Location and Planning

No matter what your situation, it takes a little planning to determine the best spot for your garden. Take into consideration where the sun tracks across the sky in relation to the space you have. Take into consideration how high you want or need your beds to be. Now, what will you eat?

Obviously, if you are a family of four and three of the four despise peas, then it wouldn't be advisable to plant a bed full of English peas, would it? You'll simply waste space. Plan things out on paper, taking into consideration what things you'd eat most and least. For many people, tomatoes are a garden vegetable that they want to give much space to. Will they grow in raised beds though? Logistics are important. We'll talk more about tomatoes and other plants like them later on.

In a traditional garden planted in rows in the ground, you'd likely have far less yield from the same square footage than you would get from raised bed gardens. This means that you can grow more by not planting in rows. Using a square gardening technique works wonders in the raised beds because you have space to walk all the way around and reach everything just fine.

The location of the sun is very important. The vast majority of vegetables will require full sunshine for at least six hours per day. If you plant your boxes in a shady area of a patio, your garden isn't going to do as well. Some seeds may not even sprout if you plant them directly into the soil. Your plants must have sunlight to grow.

If you don't have natural sunlight, it is possible to use a grow light in some circumstances. Inside a greenhouse with a grow light hanging overhead, for example, will allow you to grow your produce year-round from raised beds.

Plants that don't get enough sunlight can lead to fungi growth, insect infestations, stunted growth, and more. You need sunshine, so choose the right location and direction of your bed. Be wise when you plant things so that the taller growing plants don't leave the rest in shadows that are starved of the sunshine as well.

Do you live in a windy place? Consider a wind barrier for your raised beds if you think that your plants will be subjected to winds from summer storms or constant breezes in excess of 8 mph. This can cause plants to become uprooted and fail to thrive. Topsoil can also blow from around the roots, exposing plants that have shallow root systems to damage.

Choose a spot for your raised beds that is easily accessible to water. If you've got a 50-foot garden hose and plant your garden 75 feet from your spigot, you're not planning well. Make watering easy, and you're never going to have an excuse. Placing a sprinkler system or soaker hose on a timer can get the job done automatically. You can always override when rain is in the forecast.

Lastly, don't forget to add drainage holes to the container you build or repurpose. Soil needs to have good drainage. If not, roots will become waterlogged and can rot in place. Too much water is also an invitation to certain types of pests that will thrive and eat your plants before they have had a chance to fully mature.

Do you have a homeowner's association? These are commonly called HOAs and they are meant to provide a set of rules that will maintain the look of the neighborhood and protect the home values of anyone living there. They can also be quite restrictive and have clear rules against any gardens in the front yard. They might not allow vegetable gardens at all. Please, do check with your POA and ensure what is allowed before you go to any expense, time, or physical labor.

When determining the size of the bed, you plan to use, determine how much space you have to work with and how much room you'll want or need between your raised beds. This step is completely worth getting some graph paper, taking measurements, and drawing your ideas on paper.

Quite often, this type of planning will help you see logistical issues *before* you've done the job and wasted time, money, or physical labor. It may seem like an unnecessary step, but it's really worth slowing down and not skipping this step. After all, there is nothing worse than planting a garden to save you money and having it cost you money because the planning was all wrong.

The width of your raised bed garden should be only as wide as you can reach the middle from any side. If you are building your raised bed to be against a wall that prevents you from moving all the way around it, then you'll need to make it narrow enough to reach from the front. Check this physically, is your back happy with the reach?

A common dimension for raised bed gardening is four feet by four feet. This makes it easy to use a square foot gardening technique inside the beds, which we will talk about later on. You can reach the middle of the bed with ease for planting, watering, weeding, and harvesting. (See the Appendix for instructions to build a 4X4 raised bed.)

When deciding on the depth of your beds, you should think about what you intend to plant. Tomatoes, for example, have deep roots and like to have soil built up over their main stem as they grow. They even form roots just above the soil line that look like tiny nubs.

One of the many amazing features of a raised bed garden is that even though you may not be able to plant in the soil you have, if you leave the bottom of the bed open, the roots of the plants will find their way. Make the bed tall enough for the plants that you have, but they have a place to go without you having to dig in it.

If you pull soil up over these tiny roots that are trying to sprout from the stem, building it up an inch or so, your tomatoes will grow more roots for stability. This will help them be hardy and capable of holding more fruits. Tomatoes are heavy, the plants need to be strong and in deep soil. Tomatoes need at least twelve inches of soil under them to spread their roots adequately.

Carrots are a root plant that can grow 9 to 10 inches long, depending on the variety you choose. You have the choice of choosing a shorter variety of carrot or building boxes that are deep enough. Plan, plan, plan.

When you plan your working space between beds, make sure that you've got room for a wheelbarrow or a gardening cart. You'll need room for your own mobility but don't forget the gardening tools that you need to move around and bags of soil that need to be wheeled into your planters.

Remember that your beds can be any shape that you desire, and your garden can be put together as squares, circles, triangles, spirals or rowboats. You get to choose, so be sure that you choose what is easiest for you to work around.

A Word About Materials

Most people who build raised beds will use wood. There's an argument that happens over this constantly. Is pressure-treated lumber safe? Many years ago, the answer would be no. Treated lumber contained arsenic and also things like formaldehyde. Treated lumber today is not treated with these same types of chemicals. Therefore, yes, pressure treated lumber is safe and will not rot like untreated lumber will.

Pallets

Recycled pallets are often a free resource, and they are great. It is however important to be aware of the Information that is stamped on them regarding their safety grade. Treated pallets are not the same as treated lumber. If you are growing non-edible horticulture in your raised beds, then it probably won't make a difference (although the plants may not do as well). If you are growing vegetables or fruits in your raised beds, then this is critical.[1]

- Look carefully for the logos stamped on the pallets.
- Pallets with "MB" have been chemically treated with Methyl Bromide. You do not want this leaching into your soil.

- Pallets that say "HT" are heat-treated and safe for your raised beds.
- Ensure that in addition to "HT" the pallet says IPPC (International Plant Protection Convention)[2] The IPPC designed standards for wood packaging to prevent the spread of pests and diseases. You can trust that the pallet is heat-treated if the IPPC stamp is on it.
- We recommend that you should stay away from unstamped pallets because you don't know whether they have been chemically treated.

Dry rock walls

Consider using real rock, especially if you have rocky land. That may be the reason you need to plant raised beds in the first place. Put those rocks to good use. Do not go and take rocks from parks or along roadways. You can get a fine because they technically are owned by someone else, and parks can issue fines for the removal of rocks, wildlife, and plants as well.

One excellent use of dry rock is to put it on the outside of recycled wood. Over time, the wood will decompose, leaving you with beautiful dry rock wall raised beds. They will also provide support as the wood gets old and less stable.

Galvanized metal

Both galvanized metal containers or sheets for the walls of your raised beds are a popular choice. You should know that even galvanized material will eventually rust, some sooner than others. Other than that, this is a safe material unless you will be adding very acidic plants or materials to it. The zinc coating on the sheets will break down if exposed to acidity.

For the purists, cedar makes wonderful wood for raised beds because it is naturally rot-resistant and insect-resistant. Termites will steer well clear of cedar which means it can last for many years. This makes it very convenient, but also more expensive upfront. Weigh your options and choose what is in your budget. In the end, pressure-treated lumber is typically just fine for most people.

Kits

If you are carpentry challenged and simply want something that looks nice without scavenging materials, kits might be a good choice for you. You can spend $300 and more for these kits, and they are not overly large., but they do work great and look nice as well. You certainly could build something yourself for much less, but when you are desperate and have no tools, the kits are simple enough to put together with a screwdriver.

Some people go out and find old railroad ties. They look great, but are they safe? They're soaked in creosote. This prevents insect damage and rot. Termites even avoid it. It's toxic and poisonous. You really don't want to use that near your food. Certainly, you don't want to grow your food in a bed of earth inside of them.

Choose Your Raised Beds

As we said before, you are only limited by your needs, your space and your imagination. Here are a wide variety that you may wish to copy or use as inspiration for your own unique ideas.

The Basic Raised Bed

The most common raised beds are either 4X4 squares as mentioned earlier, or a "planter box" rectangle. The depth depends on whether you are planting something like potatoes or carrots that need depth vs herbs; or whether you just want your garden to be higher for your own convenience, comfort and accessibility.

Most people who build raised beds will use wood. There's an argument that happens over this constantly. Is pressure-treated lumber safe? Many years ago, the answer would be no. Treated lumber contained arsenic and also things like formaldehyde. Treated lumber today is not treated with these same types of chemicals and has not been since 2--3. Therefore, yes, pressure-treated lumber is safe and will not rot like untreated lumber will.

Here is an example and video tutorial of square raised beds made with recycled pallet wood.[3]

Here is a great tutorial complete with a list of materials to build raised beds with wooden frames and corrugated metal sides. [4]

Here is a good instruction guide for building a raised bed from recycled wood. [5]

And another example of using recycled wood, the instructions are here. [6]

I love this DIY tutorial. She built her raised beds for $35.00, and she did it with *cedar*![7]

NOTE: Using recycled wood is great. Also, remember that the wood needs to be untreated or pressure treated so that harmful chemicals do not leach into your vegetables. Using recycled wood is not the same as buying lumber. Someone who built with the wood may have treated it with chemicals for their purposes and are now passing it on as recycled. If you are using pallets, please see the above section that explains how to know whether your pallets are safe for your vegetable garden.

The reason that cedar is a preferred material for raised beds is that it lasts so long. Another woman figured out a way to get really cheap cedar and gives you instructions for making a cedar raised bed for $10. She is using fence pickets. Absolutely brilliant.

I used six boards to build this cedar raised bed, and spent righyt at 10 dollars in lumber (the screws will add a little to the cost)

This exact cedar planter has lasted over ten years without any issues. We have been very happy with this project and are planning on building more for our garden at our new house.

Our last curated offering for the basic raised bed is this tutorial that uses rebar for support instead of brackets or nails. He purchased untreated pine and made this for $50, building it in about an hour. [8] This one has the appeal of ease, time and money. (What's not to love?)

If you would like your own written instructions for a simple square raised bed, See the Appendix.

The U-Shaped Raised Bed

This option is also usually done with wood. You build a "U" with two longer sides and one end. The center is open for you to walk in, and you leave space to walk around the outside.

You can buy this kit for $1500: [9] If this amount of money is an option for you, then consider that you may be able to hire a local person who would do the shopping for the materials with a list and come build it for that amount of money. However, you may not have that option and building it from scratch might feel like too much, so this is gorgeous, comes with all you need, and you simply assemble it.

You can also purchase cedar, less expensive wood or source recycled pallet or other wood to build your own. Here are a couple of instruction guides:

U-Shape instructions as well as other variations on the basic idea:[10]

For $3.99 you can buy this .pdf instruction guide with materials as well as tips and tricks for building your U-shaped raised bed.[11]

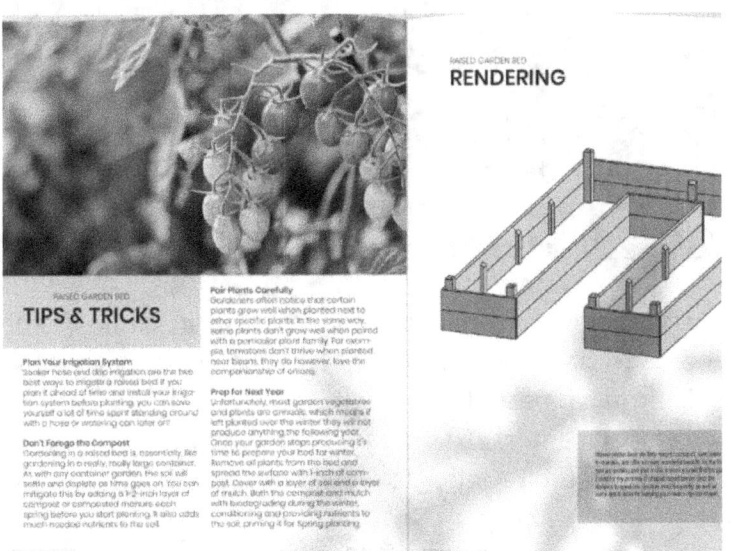

Pallet Pyramids

Pallet pyramid towers are great in a raised bed garden as a taller feature (you can put your herbs in the center of your raised bed garden in a tower, and your garden then has levels), or as a way to use side space as in the second example.

The author of this pyramid says that he spent about $200. He has used a lot of cedar for its durability and aesthetic qualities. If you wanted to, you could collect your free pallet wood over time and spend a lot less. The instructions are clear.

The basic idea of this pyramid is to make the structure/frame, cut the boards to size; then you install the boards one layer at a time while filling in with soil. The pyramid is filled with soil; they are *not* tiny individual planters. This means that your plants have plenty of room to spread their roots, grow and thrive.

Keyhole Garden

The keyhole garden is based on a design by the organization CARE (Cooperative Assistance for Relief Everywhere) in Zimbabwe. In the mid-1990's it was developed and established in many places in Lesotho because of so many people becoming disabled from the AIDS/HIV crisis. These people depended on their gardens for food and needed a way to be able to plant and tend them.[12] The arid conditions of the landscape also required a garden that was drought resistant and water efficient.

Keyhole gardens are now popular in dry places like Texas for their water retaining characteristics.[13] Although they work very well in any climate, they are especially useful for vegetable gardening in very dry places.

Features of a Keyhole Garden

You may see photos of raised beds called keyhole gardens that are circular and have a pie slice open to be able to access the garden in the center. This is a fine way to design a circular raised bed garden, but it is not what we are talking about here.

The name comes from the opening, which is not a slice of pie, but a key shape (a piece of pie with a circle in the center at the point). In the center there is a compost bin. This is where the nutrients and water soak in.

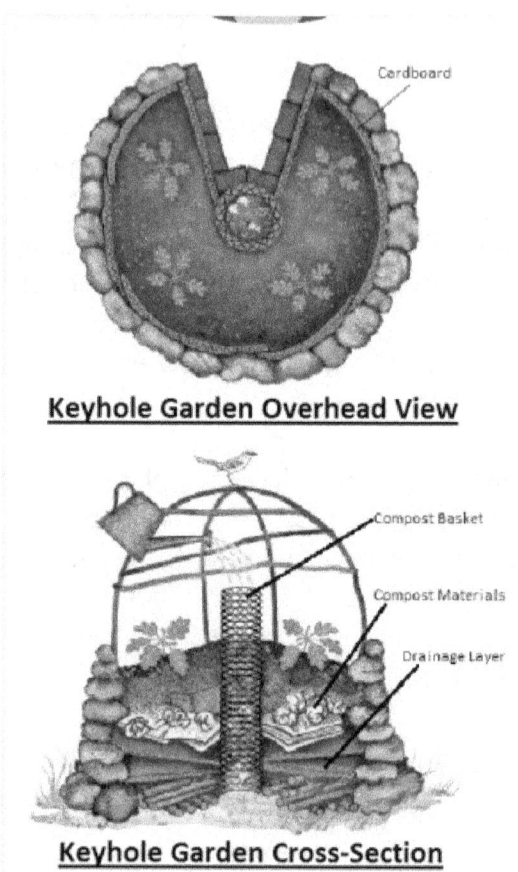

Keyhole Garden Overhead View

Keyhole Garden Cross-Section

Traditional keyhole gardens have these features as they were designed specifically with the disabled gardener in mind:
- The stone walls are high enough for a person to be able to tend them standing or in their wheelchair. These walls are built to take moisture retention into consideration as well as be strong and stable so that a person can safely lean their weight on them.

- The plants are close enough to be within an arm's reach without hurting the back.
- Even though they are relatively small gardens, they work well for intensive farming, so that many plants can thrive in a small space and offer a high yield.
- The compost bin in the center is a constant supply of nutrients to the plants at no cost.

How it Works

As well as being easily accessible to gardeners, keyhole gardens are carefully constructed and filled to retain moisture and be most efficient with soil nutrients. Below is a diagram that illustrates the layers that are set up in the initial soil. This design means that over time as the micro-organisms in the compost do their work, the soil gets richer.[14]

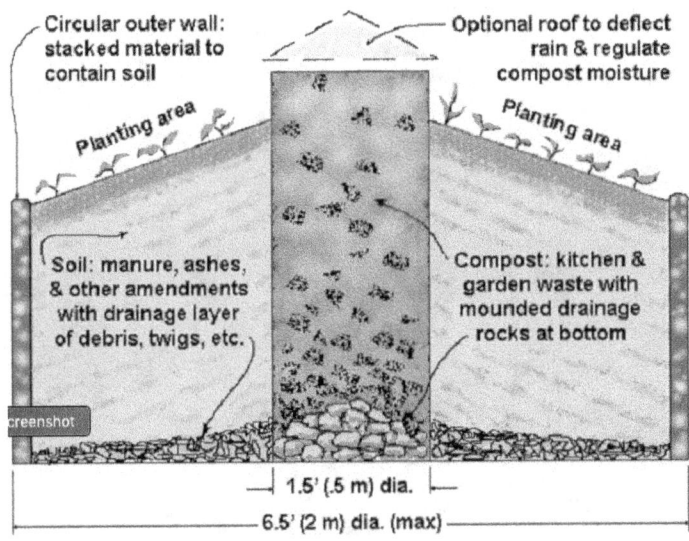

Best Vegetables to Grow in a Keyhole Garden

It is reported that leafy greens and root vegetables do very well in keyhole gardens. According to Wikipedia, "Plants with wide-reaching root systems such as tomatoes and zucchini may not perform well in a keyhole garden."[15]

How to Build a Keyhole Garden

The instructions in this footnote are the best I have seen for constructing a keyhole garden.[16] The author explains the process clearly in steps. The basic summary is:
1) Choose your location
2) Measure and mark the circle and keyhole area
3) Clear the area and prep the ground as necessary

4) Build the outer wall
5) Make the compost bin
6) Fill the keyhole garden in layers to get started

Obviously, this kind of garden takes more building effort than a lot of other raised beds. If you live in an arid climate and want to grow your own food, you may find that this is worth your while. In Africa, one of these would feed a large family for a year. There may be cost to set it up. However, since there is almost zero cost after setup, over time, the efficiency will save you money. A keyhole garden is a wonderful work of engineering and will be worthy of your time and effort.

Wood from Your Land – Sticks and Branches

If you want a rustic look that blends in with a woodland garden, and you have a lot of sticks to clean up, this is a wonderful option for a raised bed. The author says they thought of this because they needed a raised bed but had no money.

The instructions are clear, here is the summary:
- Clear your space, put weed suppressing landscape fabric down if needed
- Gather your sticks
- Gather pieces of larger branches for the corners

- Measure the height you want for the bed and cut the sticks and branches accordingly
- Build the frame
- Set in the layers of sticks
- Put in the soil and plant your garden

I would add that if you wanted to cut cardboard, pressboard or other "lining" to help keep the dirt in, you certainly could.

Squash Trellis Gardens

In a later section, we discuss trellises as accessories. We've included the trellis squash garden as its own kind of raised bed. The trellises used here are integral to the growth of the squash and because of the weight, require foundational consideration and its own approach.

If you are growing in the ground or in some kind of raised bed, you know that squashes want to sprawl. They take up a **lot** of space. One squash plant can take up 15' or even more.[17] Training them to go up solves this problem as well as being beautiful.

Growing your squash over a trellis also gives more airflow in the leaves. This prevents mildew. It also produces better-looking squashes as they don't get the brown spots from where they were lying on the ground.

What kinds of squash can grow in a trellis? Any kind, but most growers recommend that you keep the squashes that weigh more than 10lbs on the ground. There are plenty of squashes under 10lbs that will happily (and safely) reside in your trellis. A 20lb+ pumpkin is probably not a good idea to grow over your head in an arch, but the smaller, still very substantial sugar pie pumpkins work just fine.

Does it take a lot of work to get them to grow up a trellis? All it takes is a bit of observation, attention and encouragement. As they start to grow at the base, encourage the leaves through the trellis, and if you find tendrils, help them find the places best to latch on. As the plant grows, keep guiding it through the trellis and tying it to help train and support it. Twine helps give them the guidance they need.

Many squashes do not need further support after training the vines. Some require "fruit slings", which is any kind of netting to support the weight a little bit. This is a trial and error piece – some people support one squash at a time as only a few require it, others put an entire net on the underside of their trellis to support the squashes.

If you don't tend the squashes as they grow through the trellis, you can end up with a little conundrum like this:

Oops. Make sure you pull them through as they are growing.

There are many ways to trellis your squash, and we wanted to give you a range of examples. We are going to look at three categories of options based on size, effort and budget:
- Smallest – easiest - cheapest
- Medium size - easy to medium effort - medium budget
- Grander scale squash trellising adventures

Smallest – Easiest - Cheapest

Here is a DIY A-Frame arch. What wood do you have accessible to you? You can source your main materials for free and just build your arch with the cost of twine and possible screws.

The original Instagram site does not provide instructions; however, it is very simple, and you can get the idea by just looking at it. If you don't have branches accessible to build with, you could use bamboo poles.

This little A-frame arch below was made from mulberry branches collected on the author's land. You can use whatever wood you have, or purchase bamboo poles.

A variation on the A-frame squash trellis is the "lean-to". This is a great use for a pallet. You can't get easier than this! If you pick up a free pallet, the only cost would be the wire and large stables.

One gardener I spoke to in my area was saying that they wanted to make squash trellises with repurposed ladders in both lean-to and A-Frame patterns. You can see that by applying principles of strength and stability, you can either follow the patterns here or make up your own with materials that are the most easily accessible to you.

Medium Size – Medium Effort – Medium Budget

Here are some trellises that take a bit more effort and a bit more money. They also accommodate more plants and require a bit more space.

The instructions on this site are very clear, and this is a great pattern for a stable squash trellis. The author emphasizes tomato growing but indicates that it is applicable to squashes as well. The cost for this will vary depending on the wood you use. Taking the time to gather pallet wood would be the cheapest, purchasing cedar would be the most expensive.

This next squash trellis is actually medium sized and medium budget, but *easy* effort. It is strong and made to be stable for your squashes to grow and hang. The cost is $100.

This couple experimented with metal fencing they had used for a cucumber arch and found that it was not strong enough to support their squash. As a result, they cleverly designed an arch based on PVC pipe. They provide a link to purchase the step by step instructions for $5.

Grander Scale Squash Trellising Adventures

If you have the space and know-how, you may be inspired to grow squash on a larger scale. Start small and learn, then here are some inspirations to grow into.

This squash tunnel is still on an accessible DIY level; it's just larger, therefore requires more planning and design. I like the instructions in the link below the photo for this kind of arch. The size can be adjusted to what you want, the structural support and principles are the same.

This is beautiful. The simple principles are applied, just on a larger scale.

If you would like to fence in an entire garden with your squashes, you can.

This squash tunnel shown above and below is from "The Tourist Farm" in central Japan.

If you want to see more fantastic squash tunnels that will inspire you, this site has a whole list. Feast your eyes! [18]

Lastly, I want to share the best four video guides for "how to build a squash arch". If you combine the information we've discussed above with these instructions, you will be able to construct an arch, trellis or tunnel that will suit your needs, grow a high yield of yummy squashes and be a stunning feature in your garden. Find the video guides in this footnote.[19]

Raised Beds with Outdoor Seating

You can make your raised beds part of your outdoor garden design by including seating that is integral to the raised beds. This is one beautiful option. The link provides a detailed list of materials and instructions.

This next design for raised beds is built with benches along a fence line. The materials used are railway sleepers. If you choose to use this material, make sure they are **untreated** so that you do not leach dangerous chemicals into your garden. The author is in the UK and indicates a company where he can source untreated sleepers for this use.

Here is a raised bed with a seat that could be against a fence or in the center.

Corners are especially good for the mix of raised beds and seating. There is something very welcoming and cozy about sitting in a corner surrounded by plants.

If you are considering a bench option that include the benches in front of the beds, make sure that you have thought about access to tending the garden without hurting your back. In most cases if you have a kneeling pad you just lean right on over, but other designs may be more difficult. Think it for your own needs.

Add a Garden Pond to Your Raised Bed Design

This seriously raises the bar. You could make a bench *and* a small garden pond for your outdoor area.

EMPRESSOFDIRT.NET

As a quick aside: don't be put off by the idea of a pond due to mosquitos. You can purchase mosquitofish, we had them delivered by FedEx! Having thriving mosquito eating fish in our garden resulted in a *decrease* in the number of mosquitos because the environment attracts the mosquitos and the larva get gobbled up. Check out the resources here.[20]

Using Upcycled Furniture and Materials for your Raised Beds

Now, you may be more of a freegan and recycler. In other words, you like to save things and re-use them. Perhaps you dumpster dive on the weekends? It really doesn't matter what you do, as long as you're happy doing it. I have a friend in South Florida that is retired and enjoys rummaging through garbage as a hobby. She has gathered amazing garden project materials, including an old fishing net that was used to grow squash in a tunnel that could have been in Better Homes and Gardens.

I really love this dresser garden, but this is why the warning symbol is at the top of this section: If you are growing non-edible plants, then you will probably be ok. If you want to put edible plants in your upcycled materials, you have to consider whether there might be any treated wood or materials that have chemicals which will leach into your soil.

Let this dresser be an idea or an inspiration. You may have a bookcase that's ready to be retired, or like my friend, find an old fishing net. Old refrigerators can make great raised beds if you can saw through the metal layers and get the back off. The possibilities are endless.

Straw Bale Garden

Before and After Photos from Joel Karsten's website

You may have heard of this method of gardening. A horticulturist, Joel Karsten, developed it when he moved into an urban space with concrete hardscape and toxic soil. He grew up on a farm and remembered the old straw bales that would always be decomposing next to their barn. He thought he would experiment with using straw bales to grow vegetables as raised beds.

Karsten's work was featured in a New York Times article titled "Grasping at Straw" in 2013.[21] After that, the method took off like wildfire. He now teaches and demonstrates straw bale gardening globally. You can read more about his global work, including helping families and small villages be able to grow their own food in harsh conditions. You can find his website here.[22]

The "Pros" of Using Straw Bales Instead of Raised Beds with Soil

Straw bale gardening has all of the advantages of raised beds, including:
- Not having to dig in difficult or poor soil and
- having your garden raised up for ease on the back and knees of the gardeners.

In *addition* to the benefits of all raised beds, straw bales provide these advantages:

1) You don't need to purchase or acquire any building materials.
2) You don't need to build or assemble any structure.
3) Straw bales are cheap. They are only $5.00-$7.50/ea.
4) For a vegetable garden of 8 bales, you will most likely only need ½ large bag of potting soil *per year*. I also use about ¾ of a bag of blood meal per year to get the bales conditioned and about 6-10 oz of organic liquid plant food.[23]
5) You can start the planting season earlier because of the beneficial bacterial activity that composts the bales and results in heat inside.
6) Straw bales require less water than soil in raised beds.
7) They also have better drainage.
8) The bales help maintain the right temperature for the roots.
9) You get fewer weeds because the straw has no seeds in it. Very few weeds come up, and the ones that do are easy to pick out by hand.

The "Cons" of Using Straw Bales Instead of Raised Beds with Soil

With all those pluses, there can still be some downsides as you consider whether straw bales are right for you.

1) You may not like the look of straw bales. Some people get around this by using cedar (or another attractive material) to build boxes the right size to fit the bales.
   This will give you a bit more work at the end of the season. Instead of just dismantling your bales to make a great floor for your beds next year and a compost pile with the rest, you have to get the straw out of the beds you constructed. It might be easy for you to lift up the beds and get them out of the way, or you might not mind using a pitchfork or other tool to get it out. For some people, this is a "deal-breaker".

2) Since you are working with a composting process rather than soil, the nutrients take longer to absorb. If you see your plants needing plant food, you need to act quicker than you do with plants in soil. We recommend an organic liquid fertilizer so that the roots can absorb what they are lacking as soon as possible.

3) Plants like tomatoes that may not need support in the ground, or a large raised bed garden do better with support in a straw bale. I use this kind of support for tomatoes.[24]

4) A straw bale garden requires planning. With a raised bed garden using soil in boxes, you can wake up one Saturday morning and decide "I'm going to go get potting soil and plants today and plant some seedlings." With a straw bale

garden, there is a "conditioning" prep time of 12-18 days to get your straw bales ready for seeds and starts.

5) In theory, you can arrange your bales in almost any configuration, but in some instances, it might be quite a bit more work than purchasing or building a raised bed for the space. Stacking is tricky and making circles, or curved arch shapes means constructing supports to fill in the spaces where the bales meet, and you are making the curve. Bear in mind that you could have a straw bale garden in one place, and a wooden raised bed in another. By the second year, you'll have amazing compost to put into your raised beds with soil.

6) While straw bale gardening is very simple, as with any new thing, there is a learning curve. If you are an experienced gardener, then growing plants in straw bales will take some learning, attention, observation and of course...experience.

The Difference Between Straw and Hay

Don't make the mistake of getting hay bales for your straw bale garden.
Hay is grass, clover, alfalfa, barley or another plant that is cut and then bundled as bales or rolled to feed to livestock. It has the seeds and the nutrients of the plant that has been harvested.

Straw is the chafe that is leftover. It has no seeds or nutrients and is not given as feed to animals. Straw is often used as animal bedding.

Straw does not compost as fast as hay because it does not contain the nitrogen of the harvested plant.

Hay may have herbicides in it, which will not be good for your vegetable garden. [25]

If you use hay bales, you will get a lot of "weeds" in the form of the sprouts of the barley or alfalfa.

Straw does not contain any allergens. I am extremely allergic to hay and pollen. I have zero reaction to my straw bales.

Timing: When to Purchase your Bales and Set Up Your Straw Bale Garden

Ask your local straw bale source (a garden center or hardware store or local farm if you have access). Our straw comes in late summer - sometime in August. Tip: Get your straw bales then. We had to travel 2.5 hours to get straw bales when we waited too long one year in the spring. Go for the late summer after the harvest.

Set up your straw bales in the autumn. You can wait to build the supports in the spring, but at least set up the bales, level them and cover them up for the winter. The bit of extra composting will help, and they will be ready to start conditioning when spring comes.

Location

As straw bale gardening depends on thermal composting, full sun is best.

Tips for Setup

Put the cut side UP. This instruction is included in straw bale websites, videos and books, but it is easy to miss when you are learning something new. It really makes a difference. The cut side makes it easier for the plant food and blood meal to saturate the straw. The first year I had not noticed this detail and had a little trouble getting my bales conditioned. I had to tarp the bales to get them to the right temperature. Realizing my mistake, the next year I put the cut side up and *voila!* The bales conditioned like straw bale garden poster children.

Level them in the autumn, so they are not sinking slowly over the winter months. My garden is on a slope. I use rocks for support so that the bales don't lean downhill. When you uncover your bales after the winter, check the levelling before you start to condition them, so they are off to a level start.

Use supports for climbing and larger plants.
- As mentioned above, tomatoes grow really well and produce a high yield in a straw bale garden but be all the more aware of their support.
- In the "before and after" photo at the beginning of this section, you will see that there are permanent supports installed. I used this photo to make my own, and I love

them. The bales fit into it every year. They support the climbers like beans and peas, as well as aiding the support of heavy yield like tomatoes. They are sturdy for the plants, don't get pulled down and after the initial building, they are "set it and forget it".

Conditioning your Straw Bales

This is the piece that is new to those of us who have previous experience only with soil gardens. "Conditioning" means that the straw bales are decomposed enough inside. There are beneficial bacteria and microbes at work, and the straw is beginning to compost. This compost provides nutrients.

Obviously, you can't put your plants straight into straw bales from the garden center, as there are no nutrients there. This is how to condition them, so they are prepped to be a perfect environment for your seeds or starts.

Hand water with a nozzle set on "shower" for 4 days. Water each of these days until you see the water coming out of the bottom of the bale.

Day 1: water
Day 2: Apply organic, high nitrogen liquid fertilizer diluted according to package instructions
Day 3: Water
Day 4: As day 2
Day 5: Water
Day 6: As day 2
Day 7: Water

Day 8: Make sure that your bales are "hot" enough.
- A compost Thermometer[26] is handy, but not absolutely necessary. If your temperatures get between 130-145F, you will be killing off any pathogens or hitchhiking weed seeds.
- Your bales will need to be between 75-80F to plant.

Days 8-10: Water and apply ½ dose of the liquid fertilizer each of these days

Day 11: Apply 1 cup of blood meal per bale, diluted according to package direction and water

Day 12: Plant if the temperature is 75-80F.
- Let them cool if it is hotter, throw a tarp over the bales for a day or so if they are not ready.

Planting your Straw Bale Garden

If you want to start planting when it's a little early, and there is still a risk of frost, just put a plastic sheet over your starts overnight to get a greenhouse effect. Be careful about leaving it on during the day: If it is cold, leaving cover on during the day will be fine, but if it is sunny and warmer then you could burn your starts.

Planting in a straw bale is very similar to planting anywhere. You can follow the usual instructions about spacing between plants. There are some planting differences for straw bale gardening:

- If you are planting seeds, put a thin layer of seed-soil on top of the bales. Follow instructions on the seed packet for spacing as you would any other planting.
- For all starts, make space with a trowel in the straw layers. Small ones are easy. Larger ones benefit from having a

trowel with a sharp tip that can do a bit of digging. Sometimes I get the trowel down in and then turn it around and pull it out trying to scrap as much straw out as I can. This loosens the straw enough so that I then pull out the straw in the space to make room for the start.
- Put the start in the hole you've made and surround it with potting soil. Tuck it in and gently push it down, then use the straw that you took out to make the hole to press on top underneath the stem of the plant so that the potting soil is covered.
- Feed your starts as you would any other planting. A lot of gardeners like to use liquid vitamin B to support the roots and avoid shock.

Watering a Straw Bale Garden

Straw bale gardens take less water. How much water is enough? When you plant your starts, water them as you would any pot or raised bed. Watch for the water coming out the bottom of the bale like you would a potted plant. Then stop.

After you've planted your seeds and starts, a drip irrigation system or soaker hose on a timer is the best recommendation.

As a guide, in my hot summer/cooler night climate, I set my soaker hose on a timer for 40 minutes, three times a week. I turn it off and skip if there is enough rain to soak the bales, and I check the bales daily if we get high 90'sF or higher temps for days in a row.

Caring for Plants in Your Straw Bale Garden

With one exception, care, harvest and troubleshoot your plants as described for any raised bed garden.

I stated this before, but will say it again - there is one important difference for straw bale troubleshooting:
- If you see your plants turning yellow, they usually need nitrogen. As mentioned above, you need to be quick if you see any yellowing. Again, liquid fertilizer is best as the nutrients can be absorbed quicker than solid fertilizer.[27]

Autumnal Breakdown

By now you've purchased your straw bales for the next year, and they are waiting to be set up for the winter. You've enjoyed the delicious harvest of your straw bale garden for the season; it's time to roll up the soaker hoses and break down the bales. As you begin to break down the bales, separate the plant remains and form a compost pile of straw and layers of the old plants. You can let it go or encourage the rich compost action by treating it like any other browns/greens compost pile. We will describe this later in the "Lasagna Composting" section.

You can use the compost in other raised beds, and it is wonderful in the bottom of pots.

Once you've cleared the bales, made your compost pile and flattened out your garden space, you're ready to bring in the bales you've purchased to set them up for the winter. The cycle begins, and now once you've done it, the next year will have less set up and be even easier.

Hügelkultur

 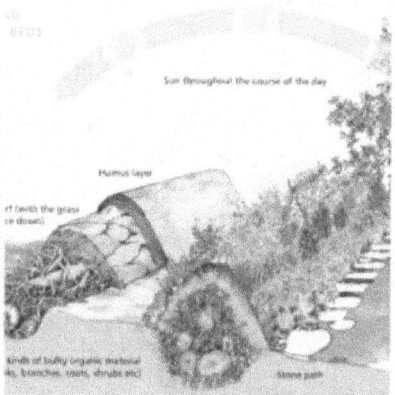

Have you heard of hügelkultur gardening? Hügelkultur is a German word meaning "mound culture" or "hill culture". It was a method of raised bed gardening practiced in Germany and Eastern Europe for hundreds of years. The first time it was mentioned as a term in a gardening book was not until 1962. [28]

The basic idea is that it is a way to replicate and accelerate the decomposition process of the forest floor by making layers of material that are rich in carbon (logs, sticks, other compostable materials) with soil and compost mixed in between. The mound is often layered into a triangular shape because it is based on logs as the wide base. The concept, however, can be shaped into a circle or a spiral, or "L" or any shape you want – you just have to chainsaw the logs into rounds. We will also discuss filling your raised beds using hügelkultur principles.

Here is a classic hügelkultur garden with multiple mounds

You can make hugels in spirals, circles or snakes as well.

Hügelkultur is a method best used in places with ample space and is ideal if you have land with trees and branches that need to be cleared or trees that have fallen.

The method I share with you here is a mix of what you can find in books and on instructional websites and videos as well as my own experience as taught by mentors. My kitchen window looks out on our hügelkultur mound at the bottom of a meadow. It is currently bursting with leafy greens.

The Benefits of Hügelkultur

- Hügelkultur is regenerative. The logs that are breaking down over many years at the bottom are becoming compost and constantly giving nutrients to soil. We plant leafy greens that seed themselves and have come up in the spring without any tending whatsoever. They don't need any fertilizer or plant food. My only tending is picking them.

- You have a longer planting season. Because hügelkultur is based on compost, there is heat. The soil is ready for planting before garden plots in the ground. This is a huge plus in places with a short growing season.

- You need much less water. When you set up your hugel, you'll need to soak the logs thoroughly so that they compost well. The first year you will need to water as you would a raised bed garden. After that, there are mentors that, you deep soak your hugel once a year. Unless there is severe drought, you shouldn't have to again.[29]

- In addition to holding moisture, the drainage and aeration is better than ground plots and raised beds with soil. It happens naturally because the soil is built around the wood (logs, branches, sticks).

We will look at two ways of building hügelkulturs: 1) On the ground and 2) in raised beds.

How to Build a Hügelkultur in a Trench or on the Ground

1) Choose your location according to your space and needs.

    If you are making the typical "triangle" shape, think carefully about how you orientate your mound. To get morning sun on one side and afternoon on the other, place your hügelkultur north to south. If you place it east to west or some other in-between configuration, consider the arc of the sun in its placement. What effect will it have?

2) Gather wood for the base and center of your hugel. There are some kinds of wood to avoid, otherwise, whatever you have on your land.

    <u>Wood to Avoid</u>:[30]
    Cedar (it breaks down too slowly)
    Redwood (also breaks down too slowly and can be toxic to other plants)
    Walnut (inhibits the growth of other plants)
    Black Locust (can be toxic to plants)
    Willow (if the willow is green it will sprout, and you'll have a willow patch. It's tenacious.)
    Any diseased tree will likely infect your garden.

3) Once you've chosen the placement and length size, then dig a 12" trench, the length of your hugel. Keep the soil from

the trench handy on the side – it will go back into your mound!

For a triangular shape, the trench needs to be wide enough to hold the two or three logs/trunks on the bottom with very little airspace in between them.

If you are constructing a circular or a mound of another shape – interpret the hügelkultur principles to your design: You want to have large logs with some air space as a base and bottom layer. The more logs, the better. The only limitations to the number of logs are your space and how many logs you have. Remember, these will be providing nutrients and moisture retention to your mound over time. This site is a good resource for lots of different hugel shapes.[31]

If you are in a place where it is rocky and impossible to dig a trench, then you can build this on the ground, you will need to consider how to make it stable. Some hügelkulturists build a simple frame with 2X4's. Here is a drawing of a hugel built on the ground. Trenches are preferable because they hold moisture to help the logs stay soaked.

raised garden bed hugelkultur after one month
Raised bed garden built up from the ground

4) Place the logs/or downed trees in the trench.

   They can be placed lengthwise like this:

Or you can stand them up in the trench like this:

Here is an example of a hügelkultur ready for soil and compost. The logs have been cut into rounds and are set upright on the ground without a trench.

5) Place layers of bush or grass clippings, but not thick enough to make the mound unstable as they quickly decompose. As you layer, it is useful to fill in the gaps with the soil from the trench, or compost. If you don't have enough soil, consider sourcing weed-free soil from a local supplier who would deliver it in a truck (or you could pick it up if you have the equipment).

The layers of clippings, etc. are for accelerating the natural composting process. It is key to remember that this is different from a garden scrap compost pile. The branches and woody material hold the moisture over a long period of time, and they also provide the nutrients. You don't want to put too many layers of other material (like grass clippings) because the Hugel will collapse.

People do say that you can make hügelkulturs based on straw. Straw will work but will also decompose and collapse after about 4-5 years. It also will not provide the nutrients that decomposing logs will. The traditional hügelkultur is using the wood to make a long-term garden bed with water and nutrients.

As you build, be aware of stability and accessibility. Some people recommend making hugels steep so you can reach the plants, but there is the issue of gravity causing soil runoff. You *do* need to be able to reach your plants to harvest them. There is a whole science regarding soil and slope angles, [32] but common sense will probably tell you what will work.

Stack intentionally. Think about there being support for soil as you build the inner foundation for your hugel.[33]

Tip: If you choose, you can purchase or gather stepping-stones to place in the garden when you build it. They just need branches for support, so they are stable. Add the stones and press them down when you have finished the top layer of the mound. Wiggle them around to make sure they are stable. This will save you stepping into the hugel and causing the soil to collapse. This takes a little planning when stacking the logs, or a bit of chainsaw work to make a level space for the stepping-stones. Make sure you don't use cinderblocks or any material that could leach toxic chemicals into your garden.

6) This is the point where it's best to soak your hugel. Get the water into the logs before the top layer of soil.

7) After the log soaking and watering of the base soil, finish your hügelkultur with a layer of potting soil, compost or just the soil from the trench (if you have any left). Then gently soak the topsoil, ensuring that it doesn't runoff.

Growing Plants and Tending Your Hügelkultur

For the most part, planting and tending in your hügelkultur is the same as any raised bed. Grow what you want, companion planting is proactive troubleshooting before the trouble starts, give support to heavy or climbing plants, watch for pests, cover if there is frost, harvest.

Considerations Unique to Hügelkulturs:

1) <u>Root vegetables might not be a good idea for the first few years</u>. They tend to be difficult to harvest without tearing apart your wood stack.

   Some people deliberately plant root vegetables for stability and leave the potatoes (or other) to compost in the hügelkultur between the layers of wood. This is fine if you intended to do that, but frustrating if you were not expecting to leave your vegetable harvest in the hugel as a compost sacrifice.

2) <u>Water is a learning curve</u>.

   <u>First Season</u>: You soak it when you build it and keep watering it the first season. Determine whether your plants need water as you would any other garden bed – with a moisture thermometer or your fingers.

   <u>Subsequent Seasons</u>: Your hugel will be retaining moisture, you may find that reseeded plants start to come up on their own accord. Soak it slowly and deeply once, then assess carefully before watering so that you don't over water.

Hügelkultur Principles in a Raised Bed Frame:

This site has good instructions for "down-sized" homesteading. Here is a Hugel getting started in a raised bed:

One of the main benefits of hügelkultur practices in raised beds is that it is a way to gradually compost nutrient-rich soil for your plants while at the same time saving a lot of money not having to purchase soil to fill your raised bed frames.

In a raised bed, you will start with smaller logs than you do with a traditional mound. Get logs that are about 5" in diameter for an average rectangle raised bed that you would buy at your hardware store for the first two layers. The logs get smaller as you layer. By the time you get to the top, you are placing sticks on the hugel.

1) Put the logs in the bottom of the raised bed
2) Layer as you would for lasagna composting but keep the logs dense.

- green grass clippings, or other "greens"
- a little straw or other "brown"
- next size down branches

Keep layering till you have 6" of room for soil at the top.
3) Soak as you would a hugel mound
4) Take this opportunity to add more soil or compost to go into the cracks
5) Put topsoil or potting soil on top, gently soak again.

This gives you benefits of a hugel mound. The first year you soak the bed deeply, then monitor water as you would normally. The second season onward you soak once a year and assess as you would any garden for moisture.

Being the "mini" version of hügelkultur, it might dry out quicker than the larger mound, but retain water more than a raised bed filled with soil. This will depend on its location. With a little observation, it won't take long to know what your plants need in their perfectly moist nutrient-rich home.

Conclusion of Hügelkultur Gardening

As I said, what I have shared with you is the theory and practice of traditional hügelkultur that I have learned from books, websites, mentors and my own experience. For all of the positive reports, experiences and instructions (including mine above); it would be remiss if I did not include criticism of the hügelkultur technique.

Robert Pavlis of gardenmyths.com raises points and concerns about the use of hügelkultur. The main points are:

- It has not been scientifically evaluated or researched. There is a lot of anecdotal evidence raving about it, but they don't offer comparisons of other kinds of gardening using the same soil, in the same year, growing the same plants.
- Building a steep slope for a garden asks for soil runoff. He suggests it's better to use this method in a low, raised bed garden.

Read the article yourself to determine whether his analysis would shift your hügelkultur plans.[34]

I will say that we have raised beds, a straw bale garden and a hügelkultur mound. I've not planted the exact same plants every year in them, but nothing is holding moisture like the hugel. Also, the raised beds and raised beds with soil around the house had the same leafy greens, and they did not spontaneously re-seed and start growing themselves in the spring whereas we are harvesting from the hugel every night to keep up with the abundance.

If you have land as well as trees that need to be dealt with, I highly recommend you consider this one option for your garden plans.

Herb Spirals

These are beautiful, fun and apply the principles of intensive gardening and Japanese philosophy to produce a high yield in a small space.

The basis of an herb spiral is a spiral that gains height as it goes to the center. The Japanese observed nature and observed that an ascending spiral would create "microclimates" in miniature. Some herbs love the sun, others partial sun, some love moister soil, others like to be watered and then drained dry. The spiral provides all of these needs in one small place. The top will get more sun and drain quicker than the bottom, which will be for plants that want more moisture consistently.

The spiral also has variances in hours of sunlight. The south side gets the most sun; the eastern side gets morning sun and the western more afternoon. The north side will have the most shade.

Many herb spirals are built with stones or brick; this too was designed because these materials warm up during the day and keep the plants warm at night.[35]

Herb spirals can be made very simply like this one:

Or they can be steeper with taller walls and deeper soil.

If you don't have a lot of stones handy, you can use bricks

Flat landscaping rock makes a lovely herb spiral

You don't have to use stones you can find other materials.

All of these photos are from the same site. They give many options for herb spirals and offer plans for the plants as well as the design and construction. [36]

There are other sites with instructions and various plans as well. The Garden Channel has a video about making an herb spiral that is a planter with a stone wall held by cement. Obviously, this is a bigger project, but you can tell that this will last and look how easy it will be to access the entire garden.

I especially like the photos of preparing the ground and the first steps on this website. He also offers a map of the herbs from a ground level view, not just a helicopter view.

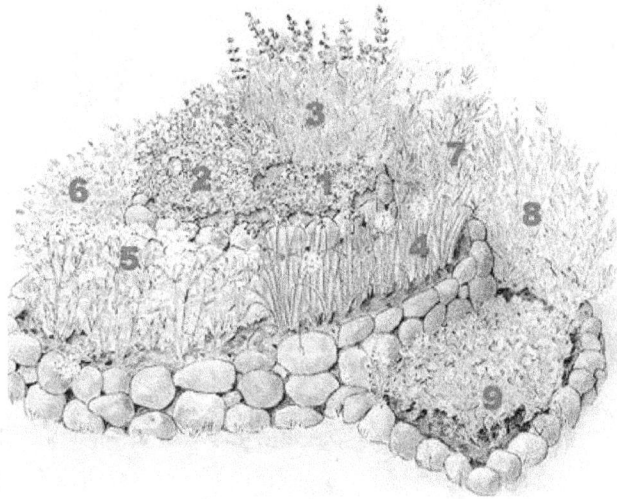

Here is a very compact little herb spiral. The author gets the support for the stones with wire mesh.

Planters and Herb Gardens

Let's "go small" for a moment. We've looked at farm size squash tunnels, hügelkultur made with whole tree trunks, straw bale gardens and raised beds with benches and garden ponds (to name a few).

The small planters and raised beds for herb gardens are not to be ignored. But have you ever gone shopping to buy them? They are *very* pricey. Small planters may be all you do for your edible garden, or they could be a part of a grander landscape plan.

This herb garden did not come in a kit. It is DIY, and the link below the photo will show you how to make it. There are helpful diagrams as well as photos in his woodshop as he is making it. Small L-shape raised beds like this can give a patio or deck an elegant feature.

This herb wheel is another DIY project with a free plan. The graphics are well done and make understanding easy.

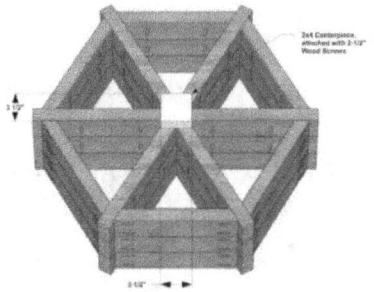

You might choose to have various small planters with legs to raise them to a height that is right for the space or right for your body to make it easy to grab your herbs while you are cooking.

This one is a larger example, but it is included here because the construction is well described and sound, as well as well-built for both drainage and moisture retention.

You can "mix and match" the insights of "Grandmas House DIY" along with the plans to make smaller raised planter boxes such as these:

This is the simplest DIY small raised planter – it is described as being "for kids", which is great, but I can see this being a design that could fit in a number of places throughout a garden or a patio.

I personally love coming out to a tiered herb garden to collect my fresh herbs as I cook. They are all together in one place, look welcoming while giving elegance to a patio or deck. Purchasing these planters can be ridiculous in price, and many are not well built. This one has good instructions, and it will be built to last if you follow the instructions.

There are many ways to design and accommodate small planters for herbs in any size space. The key is to step back and think:

- How close do I want the herbs to be to the house? Do I want them to be right outside the door because I harvest them when I cook? Do I tend to harvest them when I'm harvesting other vegetables?
- How much space do I need for my herb garden?
- How would planters fit into the design of my outdoor space? Where would I put them? Do they fit well in the space I have with the furniture or raised beds already in place?

When you have answered these questions, you can choose your small planter boxes and place them where they will fit in to your garden or outdoor area.

Raised Bed Options We Do Not Recommend

You will see people out there recommending building raised beds with these materials, but we do not recommend them and here is why:

⊘Old Tires

Sometimes it is the thinking outside of the box that makes your project the most successful. As mentioned earlier, you may use any type of container of the correct size for your needs to create a raised bed garden. Some people have created small raised beds with old tires. Are they safe, though?

Two schools of thought exist on using tires. Some people feel that the petroleum in the tires will leech into your soil and find its way into your food. Not good. What does research on this say? The answer, apparently, is yes *and* no. Your used tires are safe to use for one or two seasons.

After that, they begin to biodegrade, and that is when you must worry about the leaching of chemicals. Zinc, carcinogenic PAHs (polycyclic aromatic hydrocarbons) and other toxic compounds are found in the materials that tires are made from. So actually, petroleum is the least of your worries.

The bottom line with tires is that if you are looking for a long-term garden idea, save them for other things that don't involve food. Dispose of them properly. Understand that they pose a threat to your health when they breakdown. They also heat the soil very quickly and would likely not be suitable for most plants.

⃠Cinder Blocks

Another popular material that is used by people in raised bed gardening that is questionable would be cinder blocks. Frankly, these are made with materials that can also leach into your soil and your food.

The first thing that you need to investigate is if your blocks are cinder or cement. Cement blocks are made with Portland cement and with other material that is crushed aggregate. They are much heavier than cinder blocks and cost more too.

Cinder blocks are also made with the same type of cement, but it is mixed with fly ash. That's a by-product of the coal industry. This makes them lighter. They are cheaper too.

The coal ash is a huge problem though. It's a by-product of burning coal for power in electric plants. It is collected and sold for the cinder blocks. It is similar to the cement and therefore substituted for a portion of it to create blocks that weigh less, aren't as structurally sound, and are filled with toxic material.

Coal contains heavy metals and toxic materials. The ash contains traces of these

The coal itself contains many heavy metals and other substances known to be toxic. A considerable amount of these metals and substances remain in the ash. They are subsequently found in the cinder blocks that are created from it.

When you use these to outline a raised bed, the potential of leaching these toxic materials and metals into your food is very real. The impact of these materials has been identified as the cause of nervous disorders, cognitive impairment, and a higher risk of cancer. It's simply not in your best interest to use blocks to line your garden.

Instead of cinderblock, it may be more in your best interest to consider using real rock, especially if you have rocky land. That may be the reason you need to plant raised beds in the first place. Put those rocks to good use. Do not go and take rocks from parks or along roadways. You can get a fine because they technically are owned by someone else and parks can issue fines for the removal of rocks, wildlife, and plants as well.

⊘Old Railroad Ties

Some people go out and find old railroad ties. They look great, but are they safe? They're soaked in creosote. This prevents insect damage and rot. Termites even avoid it. It's toxic and poisonous. You really don't want to use that near your food. Certainly, you don't want to grow your food in a bed of earth inside of them.

Accessories and Add-ons for Your Raised Beds

Some plants will require that they have something to help them grow, such as a trellis to climb on. Tomatoes need cages to help support them when they grow heavy and large. You can add these to your beds with some simple adaptations.

Cages

Cages can be purchased or made from wire fencing and wrapped around your plants, clipped together at each end by bending the wires over like loops to hold each side together and they'll form a cage that will protect your plants as they grow and provide them with support.

Here is a tomato cage from Lowe's that costs $2.98.

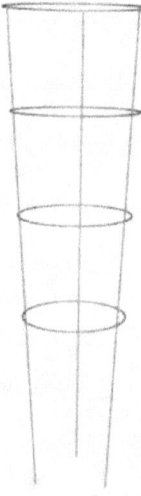

This cage is great if you are growing one or two plants, but if you have a large tomato garden, then even $3/ea. adds up fast. Also, some gardeners find that these cages are not heavy duty enough to support their tomatoes.

Here are some DIY options for tomato cages

This is a clear video demonstration of how to build a very easy wire cage 5' tall with a roll of wire garden fencing. The 5' tall, 50-foot roll of fencing would be about $66 and would make about 12 cages. It is clear that this cage will be sturdy enough to hold heavy tomatoes and also allow room for getting your hands through to tend and harvest. You can roll them up and store them offseason as well.

If you want to build permanent wooden tomato cages, there are a lot of DIY ideas and instructions. These are simple and relatively inexpensive, while being elegant and attractive.

Wood or bamboo will tend to be much more expensive, but certainly beautiful and durable. I've collected some of the best in this footnote.[37]

Trellises

A trellis can be added to the back of a box to allow for something to climb. Alternatively, they can also be constructed as an arch over the bed(s) or a variety of other ways. Varieties of beans and peas prefer to climb, and trellises can be made for them easily. Whether you use wire to create a tunnel over your bed that your gourds can grow on, or you use some latticework to make a trellis, none of these are difficult or expensive. In fact, you can use tree limbs trimmed from trees to form a trellis, bending them and wiring them together into whatever creative shapes that you'd like.

Remember that melons and some gourd varieties can grow quite large and be heavy. You'll want to provide very strong support for them, and that is likely going to be made of wood. You could use a cattle panel, which is a very heavy gauge fence, sometimes called a hog panel, and it can be bent into an arch that will support quite a lot of weight. It's also an inexpensive option with no building skills required. See the squash trellis section for growing these kinds of heavier fruits and vegetables.

If you want a great tutorial in building a wood trellis for the back of your raised beds next to a fence, this one is excellent.

If your raised beds are not against a wall or fence, this video will show you how to make a solid but inexpensive trellis that surrounds your beds on three sides.

Trellises are not limited to being at the back of a raised bed or circling around a plant or as an arch. They can also be in the middle of a bed, accessed by plants on both sides.

It doesn't have to be expensive or difficult to make a tunnel you can walk through. This trellis is beautiful, made of natural wood from their land.

If you want to make your trellis for under $5 this is the way to go.

Wire arches are also a way to use trellises on your raised beds. One of the many benefits of using wire as a small arch over the top of your raised bed is that you can also now use that as a frame to put plastic over your plants. This creates a quick mini greenhouse to prolong your growing season by as much as two to three months, depending on where you live.

If you need a frost cover, a layer of breathable fabric over the arch you've already got in place will warm your plants close to 15 degrees over the air temp around them, saving them from an early frost in fall or a late frost in spring. I have vivid memories of the next-door neighbor covering her large garden with every sheet she owned.

You can make a large wire arch over a number of beds to grow sun loving plants on the trellises over the arch and create a shade garden in the bed(s) underneath.

You can also make wire arches over each bed.

You can see that like your raised beds, your trellis options are only limited by your needs and creativity. If you see an idea you like but the shape doesn't fit, chances are you will be able to adapt the principles to work for your space.

Go to this footnote for more tutorials and DIY instructions for building trellises. Be inspired! Think about what will be best for your plants and your space.[38]

Incorporate a Greenhouse

If you need a little extra warmth even in the summer, this is an easy and affordable DIY project.

This next greenhouse setup is larger, but not that difficult to make. Have you ever seen plastic sheeting look so good? Note: You wouldn't have to be covering squares this big. This could be done with any size of raised bed.

This photo is from the site in this footnote.[39] Unfortunately, the link provided for instructions for building this leads to an unrelated site. It looks like they are made with gazebo frames.

Other Accessories
- A Wood platform under your raised bed
  This is visually lovely with two major benefits: 1) If you have dense clay or other soil that does not drain well, it is very useful for keeping your raised bed from retaining too much water. 2) If you have moles that may burrow up into your garden from below, this will stop them without preventing drainage. This platform can be made with some of the zero or low-cost materials we have discussed (like pallets or fence stakes), or you can measure the dimensions you want and make your own.

- Landscape fabric
    - Landscape fabric is often used to cover the ground underneath your raised bed to suppress weeds. You can get a wide range of grades from light and less cost to more expensive "pro" level. See this footnote for an example of your choices. [40]
- Plastic Sheeting
    - Plastic sheeting can extend your growing season and protect your plants from late spring or autumnal frosts.

I get sheeting that is heavy enough to drape over metal fence posts without tearing. [41]
- Bird netting
  - Fruit trees and berries are most known to have problems with birds, but some gardeners find that protection over their raised beds is useful for their area. This footnote will show you a couple of examples.[42]

Fencing

What do you need to fence out? Are you fencing out a small dog or a toddler? Perhaps you need something taller than that, but for a small garden. I once had squirrels who would dig spirals in my raised beds, are you fencing out squirrels? If you are fencing out deer, you need either an enclosure around a small raised bed garden or a taller fence or dual perimeter.

There are many ways to fence an entire yard. For this guide, we are focusing on protecting raised bed gardens specifically.

We are going to look at some fencing options small to large.

Small Scale Fencing for Raised Beds

This kind of added fence is enough if you are discouraging dogs, cats or toddlers from digging in your raised beds. The builder calls it a "pest gate", and it is removable so you can reach your plants with ease. It doesn't have to be this short; his instructions allow for making it taller if you want to.

If you need more than the "pest gate", this would be the next level up. If you have just a couple of raised beds but you need taller fencing around them, this is the easiest way to do it. Her instructions include a way to make it easy to get in and out.

Medium size Enclosures for Raised Beds

If you want to enclose several raised beds in one place, this is a basic, well-built option that includes a screen on top to keep out birds. The space in the center is for access, surrounded by three beds. There are step by step instructions written clearly.

You may want an enclosure that is more than basic and has a few more visual features. This one is beautiful, and it is DIY.

Large Scale and Deer Fencing

If your raised bed area is larger than the previous examples, then you may want to look into fencing for larger perimeters. These next suggestions will focus on fencing larger areas than three beds and keeping out the dreaded predator of every yummy plant: deer.

> *"...Deer have total amnesty. They walk through your yard like supermodels on hooves."*
> *- Robin Williams* [43]

Oh yes, indeed they do! I have watched a lot of deer, and quite a few deer jumping fences. There is conflicting information from experts about how high a deer fence should be. I've seen some governmental organizations say that a 4' fence is enough to deter most deer. Not the deer I know.

Alamy Stock Photo has a lot of photos of deer flying over fences

You get the idea. My own observation of deer and fencing is this:

Height of fence	Response of Deer
4'	"Annoying, but "doink!" right over it
5'	"OK...hup!" - over in a flash
6'	"Focus...don't blow it...nice run up...huuuuh-yah!"
	"Phew! Up and over, now for the lettuces."

I've not seen a deer jump a 7' fence, and I think this is an unusual feat. A 7' fence is a very big and expensive thing to build. You also may not enjoy something that tall in or around your yard.

If you are building a deer-proof fence around an entire yard that includes a vegetable garden, ask around about what other people do in your neighborhood. You may not need a 7' or 7.5' fence. You may also decide to put a 4' fence around your yard to keep out local dogs and cats, and deter people, but put some other kind of fence around your raised beds inside.

Here is a site that offers specialized "Deer, Orchard and Wildlife" Fencing[44]

<u>Fencing to Avoid in Deer Country</u>

It is worth noting that it is important to choose fencing that will not injure or even kill the deer. Hunting is one thing, a deer dying an unnecessary slow torturous death is another.

- <u>Don't use barbed wire.</u>
  It's great for keeping in cattle, but deer can't see well enough to know it's there or understand that there are barbs on the top if they jump it. Deer can actually run right through it and get tangled. A Forest Service worker in Montana reported that it was common to see dead fawns that had been caught in a barbed wire fence. [45]

  Many cattle ranchers have barbed wire fences in deer country, and any other option would be unaffordable for the amount of acreage they are enclosing. If you do have a barbed wire fence where deer are crossing, you can put flags or cloth or twine from bales and hang it on the barbed wire. It will let the deer know a fence is there so they won't run right through it, and it can also spook them a bit when it moves in the wind.

We've talked about using wire mesh fencing for various options such as the dual perimeter. Make sure that the mesh is small enough so that they won't try to get their head through it. Even if you don't purchase fencing from the experts, you can take their lead.[46]

- <u>Don't build fences with spikes on top.</u>
  The deer can get ripped along their underbelly or impaled.

- <u>Don't use fencing with a decorative bar or other feature underneath the top</u>.
  Some fences have an extra bar at the top of the fence about 6" underneath the top support. Deer can get their foot caught in these, break their leg and be stuck hanging.

Next we are going to look at electric fencing and dual perimeter fencing. These last two options discussed are intended for enclosing multiple raised beds either on land with no other fencing or inside a large yard that is surrounded with a lower fence.

<u>Electric Fencing</u>

If you are building a 7.5' fence, electric mesh fencing is an initial expense of about $350/100 feet. The beauty of it is that it is both effective *and* you can roll it up outside of the growing season, so you don't have to look at it or maintain it all year. The site in this footnote specializes in deer damage control and offers fencing kits.[47]

Some kits come with solar panels or offer them as optional extras.

Common knowledge amongst gardeners and some governmental or university sites is that deer don't see well over 7 feet, so they recommend 7.5 feet in height. Point taken, but that's a *lot* of fence. On the other hand, Iowa State University Extension says this:

> *Short electric fences can be effective in discouraging deer from entering small patches or gardens but need to be tall or angled to prevent entry into larger (more than 100 square feet) patches. The number of strands necessary to deter deer can vary depending on how motivated the deer in the area were. Applying thinned peanut butter to synthetic fence at deer nose height can increase effectiveness, as deer will learn quickly that the fence is electrified.*[48]

I love the *"peanut butter at nose height"* trick. If you decide on electric fencing, determine the skill and motivation level of your local deer. Also consider the run-up they have, and how much room is inside the fence. You don't want to spend more money than you have to, but you *do* want it to be effective.

An electric fence may not be the right choice for you due to the inaccessibility of power or the cost of the battery or solar power supply. Also, an electric fence is obviously not a good choice for surrounding raised beds in a yard where young children might be playing.

Here is another option for enclosing multiple raised beds and protecting them from deer:

Dual perimeter fencing

This is the kind of fencing that I chose to enclose my straw bale garden.

The idea of dual perimeter fencing is that with two fences, the deer either don't want to try to jump it because they can't interpret what they are seeing or if they do, they will get inside the first one and not have the room to get over the other. You then let them out, and they don't come back.

Our inside perimeter is 5.5 feet tall; the outside is 5 feet tall.

The supports are metal fence posts.
The fencing itself is wire mesh.
"Gates" are made by cutting the wire and simply bending the edges around the fence.

The photo below is a close-up of an open gate.
We cut the wire so that pieces stick out at the ends, then bend them as "hooks" so that they can latch into the wire mesh.

Here is the closed gate. Look closely and you can see the wire "hooks" made from just cutting and bending them. They are wrapped around the fencing. It has been easy to open and close and no child or deer has figured it out, or been injured trying.

The fences are three feet apart inside. We have never had a deer try to get in. They come up to the fence and stare into the vegetable garden longingly. In fact, *when I took these photos,* there was a deer doing exactly that. She is looking at my vegetable garden now! (I'm not kidding, she was right there.) She, nor any of her multiple friends or family have tried to jump this.

Neighbor staring at my vegetable garden with thievery on her mind.

I have a friend in the area who has a dual perimeter fence like this, but a larger garden. His fences are 5' and 6' high and occasionally one will get over the first fence. They don't have enough room to get over the second one, so they are trapped until you let them out.

If you don't like the looks of these options, Houzz published an article titled *"Yes, a deer fence can be decorative"* featuring beautiful designs for fences. Be inspired or take a look and hire a contractor. Here are three of many examples, these are truly stunning.

Even if you can't manifest gardens or fences on this scale, it is always useful to look at the ideas and the engineering of these constructs. The principles can scale down to what you are building. One of the features that this article highlights is the use of pagodas (the tops that stick out flat, towards the outside) to deter deer.

Decide for yourself what the best option might be to protect your raised beds. If you only have a few beds to protect, then of the first methods in this section will suffice. If you are deciding between electric fencing and dual perimeter fencing, you might consider whether you would rather be able to take down the fencing and roll it up or put up something permanent so you don't have to deal with it ever again. You also have to consider the power supply and cost.

Part Two:
Create Perfect Soil

Creating the Perfect Soil

No matter what you plant, the soil you are planting in is what will make or break your garden. That said, when you are determined to grow food, you needn't be stopped by living in a clay and rock wasteland. Raised bed gardening allows you to start with a clean slate and create your soil and your desire.

To begin with, you should understand that the best soils are aerated, have good drainage, and are relatively alkaline to neutral, being around 6.0 to 6.9 on the pH scale. 7 is the middle of the pH scale and considered neutral. Even more important, your soil needs to have the proper nutrients to support the plants growing in it and depending on it for food and nutrition.

Soil
- Provides insulation from heat and cold
- Supplies water
- Provides nutrition
- Gives support to the roots and plant stem
- Plays a key role in photosynthesis in supplying nutritional support

Without the soil healthy, plants simply cannot survive. It is a codependent relationship, you could say.

The three key nutrients in gardening are:
1. Nitrogen
2. Phosphorus
3. Potassium

There are other nutrients in the soil that are important, but these are three key nutrients that can make or break your garden. When you rely on your own soil, it may lack key ingredients for the health of your plants.

A substance added to your soil via compost, topsoil or other materials is called a "soil amendment". Let's look at ways to amend your soil to ensure it is the best for your raised bed garden.

Lasagna Composting for Raised Beds

This is a composting technique that sounds tasty, but alas, it's a visual image and metaphor rather than anything to do with a yummy pasta dish. It is also known as "sheet mulching".

The plus side of this method is that you have an easy way to compost a good amount of green garden waste as well as possibly some food scraps.[49] It's easy and requires no tending or aerating.

The downside is that it takes time – not *your* time, but a *length* of time to decompose. Ideally, you build your raised bed and start your lasagna compost in the autumn. Then you can plant six months later in the spring. Also, depending on the depth of your raised bed, you will still need 3-10" of topsoil or potting soil on top when you are ready to plant your seedlings.

The principles of lasagna composting have been used by people across the planet over many generations.

If you are a composting beginner, the basic idea is that food scraps, fresh green garden waste and dry material turn into compost through microbes breaking down the materials over time. In order to do this, the three major pillars are: 1) oxygen, 2) water and 3) the right carbon/nitrogen ratio (called the "C:N ratio") Too much carbon and you will just have dry stuff without nutrients. Too much nitrogen and you'll have a smelly raised bed.

The "lasagna" image comes from the flat layering in this composting method. To get the right C:N ratio in your raised bed, you'll be making layers with 2 parts "browns" to 1 part "greens". "Browns" are dry, carbon-rich material like flattened cardboard, paper or dry leaves. "Greens" are nitrogen-rich food scraps or fresh green garden waste.

Here's how it works:
1) After building your raised beds with an open bottom: Lay down flattened cardboard as the base. Cardboard is ideal, but if you have none, then use 5-10 layers of flattened newspaper. This base suppresses weeds and holds moisture while also allowing adequate drainage.
2) On top of the layer of cardboard, place a layer of browns with lots of air around them, such as crumpled newspaper, sticks, and dry leaves. This should fill 1/3 of the raised bed. The top inch should be the straw, dried leaves, wood chip

or sawdust. Peat moss is also considered a "brown" and works for this top layer of the base.
3) Give the whole base layer a spray of water – not to get it "wet", but to make it "moist".
4) Now add a couple of inches of either compost or, decomposed manure (if accessible to you).
5) Now for the "greens". Add your grass clippings, green garden trimmings, salad or any vegetable scraps that will not attract animals. This layer should be about 4" in a standard size raised bed.
6) Assuming your greens layer was 4", cover it with 8" of browns. Straw, sawdust, peat moss, wood chip, dry leaves are all great for this purpose.
7) Keep your raised bed covered so that the bed does not get dried out or soaked by rain.
8) Keep repeating the layers: compost (or decomposed animal manure), greens and browns until the raised bed is full. Give it a spray to moisten every time you add the browns on top. Remember the ratio is 2 parts browns to 1-part greens.
9) When it's full, water it and cover for the winter. Let it decompose till spring.
10) As the materials decompose over the winter, you'll find that they shrink. When you open it up in the early spring (or during the winter, depending on your climate), you can add some layers to get it to fill back up to about 2/3-3/4 full.
11) When you're ready to plant your seedlings, add 6" of topsoil on the top. If you include bloodmeal, compost or another soil amendment this will enrich the soil and give your plants a supercharge.

12) Now that you've done it, when the growing season is over, you can just layer some airy browns first, then compost/manure, greens and browns to start the process over.

If you are willing to wait 6 months before planting, this is very easy, and much cheaper than filling your entire raised bed with soil. It has more air, beneficial microbes and holds more moisture and nutrients as well.[50]

Other ways to Find Good Soil

You can find good soil in a few different ways. You can, and should, start composting your garden scraps immediately. This will ensure that you've got good soil to add to your garden bed each year. If the lasagna composting directly into your raised beds does not work, you can make a browns and greens pile outside.

That won't help you in the initial setup of your raised beds so here are some options to help you get that first garden planted:

- Purchase topsoil by the truckload and have it delivered to you. This is also a very inexpensive option for a lot of good dirt at once. You can use it from a pile and fill your beds as you go. Keep your pile covered with a tarp and weigh it down with some rocks so that errant weeds and grasses don't blow seeds into your pile and it won't drain away when it rains. Clarify that the topsoil you are getting is weed-free.

- Buy bags of soil. You can mix topsoil with cow manure and add a mix of whatever you feel will be the best mixture for your area and needs. You can choose to use something that is pre-fed so that you can drop your plants right into it as soon as you've filled your planters.

- Find someone who has good topsoil for sale locally. There are often people on Craigslist who are selling loads of dirt. Just be sure you aren't getting fill dirt that is poor and can have all sorts of garbage and contaminants in it. Also, ensure that it is weed-free otherwise you may have unpleasant surprises.

- If you are on a tight budget and your yard has decent dirt, you can skim the grass off the top, and then dig up some dirt from your yard if you need to. This can reduce the amount of soil you'll have to purchase later and you can add bags of potting soil to it and mix it together as you go or mix it on top of a tarp in the yard before placing it in the raised bed. This will save you from trying to mix it in the boxes, which is difficult.

- If you are creating your own mix, it's a great idea to add some peat or vermiculite to ensure that your soil won't compact too tightly and cause drainage issues or bind the roots of your plants. Ideally, the soil will be loose and easy for them to stretch out in.

- Some people contact their local landfill. They may have suitable composted soil that you can get. Many municipalities sell composted soil that they have from all the yard clippings they've picked up on lawn refuse days. Sometimes, you can even get this for free or at a very low cost. This soil may have issues of contaminants and chemicals. Ask questions about what's in it and decide whether you are comfortable with the answer.

A Math Lesson

In order to know how much soil you need, you'll have to do a little math. Multiply the length by the width of your raised bed. Let's say you are using a 4-foot by 4-foot bed that is 10 inches deep.

EXAMPLE:

4 x 4 = 16 square feet
Each inch of depth is equal to .08 feet
Therefore 10 inches x .08 = .8 feet
16 square feet x .8 feet = 12.8 cubic feet of soil to fill your box.

You can add the sum for all your boxes together to come up with your total needed. The cubic feet of soil will be listed on the labels of any bagged soils you purchase, and you can tell someone how many cubic feet you need for delivery. They'll likely convert that to cubic yards, but you can also do that by taking your cubic feet and multiplying it by 0.037037.

EXAMPLE:
12.8 cubic feet x 0.037037 = .47 cubic yards, or half a cubic yard of soil.

What About Worms?

The purpose of adding worms is to keep the soil loose, aerated, and rich in nutrients. Worms do not have to be in your raised bed gardens, but they are surely a wonderful addition.

Either earthworms or red wigglers can be used for raised bed gardening. Earthworms go down very deep into the soil, so if you have a shallow bed, they will disappear below and not do much good.

Now That You've Got It Right, Keep It That Way

Your soil isn't something you can completely ignore. Once your garden is in place, you'll still need to check your beds for signs of mold that may be an indication of not enough drainage. You'll watch your plants carefully for yellowing that may indicate too much water, or drying out from not enough.

When you've got weeds trying to come up, pull them right away. Make sure to grasp it firmly at the base of the stem and pull up firmly and slowly. The more of the root you get, the less likely it will be to come back. Some weeds have very deep taproots. The taproot is one long, central root that grows straight down.

Dandelions have taproots and so do many other weeds. This taproot will grow deep to connect them to water, and this is why they are very difficult to kill. They'll grow in places that nothing else can or will.

You should also check your soil pH periodically because growing plants and rain can change your pH levels. A soil pH tester is very inexpensive and available at most big-box retailers or order one online and get it delivered. They're usually less than $10 and well worth the investment. Periodic checks will clue you in on issues before they kill plants.

Soil that is too acidic can be treated to lower the pH. Alkaline soil can be treated to increase pH levels. When your soil is higher than necessary, a common treatment is bagged lime that is a powdered nutrient that will make your plants thrive. It's a great way to green your lawn as well. You'll want a spreader to apply it evenly.

When you initially fill your beds, make sure that you fill them to the top so that water doesn't pool at the top where it meets the sides of the box. If you overfill them, your soil will run onto the ground each time that it rains. Also, slightly mound your soil so that your center is higher and gently slopes to the edges. This will ensure that your boxes are flooding in heavy rainfall.

All of the aforementioned things can happen over the course of a few days. It's very important to check your beds daily if only to look them over and water them if necessary. You should deadhead some of your produce by gently pinching the top of the plant off and encouraging it to spread out and get thicker below. Tomatoes sometimes need this as they are growing.

Watch for bugs each week as well. A horned worm can damage tomato plants overnight, cutting large holes in the leaves. Watch for signs of insects that could be in the soil. When your plants turn color, and the water levels and pH levels are right, the first suspect is an insect. Holes in the leaves mean you've got a predator of sorts. Cabbage, for example, will fall prey to cabbage moths that eat holes in your plants and heads.

You can also purchase a kit that will check your soil for nitrogen, potassium, and phosphorus. These kits will cost between $20 and $35, depending on where you purchase yours. This will let you know when you need to add something that is essential nutrition for healthy plants. Corn, for example, needs plenty of nitrogen in order to thrive and form healthy ears of corn.

You may need to add fertilizer and you can choose organic options. For pest control, you can also find many nonchemical options to keep your garden safe to eat. Diatomaceous Earth, commonly referred to as DE, can be found at any garden center. Dusting your beds with this powder will evict and destroy any insect with an exoskeleton. If you prefer a living solution, setting these praying mantises loose is also a great option. They'll kill anything they can get a hold of.

Some flowers are wonderful insect deterrents. Consider planting them at the edges of your container or near it in other planters. Marigolds, lavender, petunias, basil, lemongrass, eucalyptus, and Chrysanthemums are excellent things to plant to keep insects away. They'll also make your garden area colorful and/or a spot for herbs as well. A planter full of mint will smell good to you but drive away many types of insects. Eucalyptus can be grown, and almost every insect despises it. Even fleas are repelled by eucalyptus.

It's important to make organic choices for yourself and your family but also for honeybees. Chemicals applied to kill weeds will be gathered by honeybees and taken back to the hive, where it can kill hundreds and sometimes entire hives of bees. This is a devastating loss because bees are in a lot of trouble. They're endangered, and we need them desperately to pollinate many of our foods. You can do your part by not spraying harsh chemicals known to kill honeybees.

If you need help with any issues, you're not able to solve on your own, consider contacting your local county extension office for the United States Department of Agriculture (USDA). They know their business and can be an enormous source of information. They might even be willing to test your soil if you've got a problem that you can't figure out on your own. You can contact them <u>here</u>.

Now that you've got your soil under control, it's time to figure out what you'll grow in your garden.

Part Three:
Choose Your Plants and Maintain Your Garden

Choosing the Right Plants

When it comes to choosing plants, as we mentioned previously, you should choose things that you'll eat regularly. Choose items that have several uses. Cucumbers can be made into pickles, stored with onions and some other ingredients to make a cold salad that is ready to eat in the refrigerator all summer long, and fresh on a salad.

You can grow virtually anything in a raised bed garden. It's simply a matter of making sure that your soil is deep enough for the roots of what you want to grow. Tomatoes like deep soil. Growing them in a raised bed requires 10 to 12 inches of soil for them to be happy. They're great food to grow.

Tomatoes can be used to create pizza marinara, homemade pasta sauces, stewed tomatoes that can be canned for recipes, sliced on salads, sandwiches, and eaten alone, perhaps with a little salt. If you hate tomatoes, there's not really much point in planting them is there?

So, make your list and then another thing to consider is how these can be stored. Will they keep at room temperature? If so, for how long? Here's a cheat sheet for a few common produce selections:

- Avocado - 4 to 7 days at room temp
- Broccoli - 7 to 14 days in the fridge
- Carrots - 3 to 4 weeks in the fridge
- Cucumbers - 1 week in the fridge

- Garlic - 3 to 6 months at room temp
- Most lettuce and leafy greens - 1 week to 10 days in refrigeration
- Onions - 2 to 3 months at room temp
- Potatoes - 3 to 5 weeks in a pantry
- Strawberries - 3 to 5 days in the fridge
- Tomatoes - 1 week at room temp
- Watermelon - 7 to 10 days in the fridge
- Zucchini - 4 to 5 days in the fridge

This is a short list to give you an idea of the huge difference in how some things can be stored. Onions keep for a long time. This means that they are a good crop to plant a lot of, keeping in mind that you can plant enough to last your family for a solid 2 to 3 months after harvesting. You can also dehydrate them to last longer if you so choose.

Zucchini, on the other hand, has a short shelf life and isn't a veggie that you will be able to can in most cases. You could potentially stew zucchini with tomatoes and can that as a soup. It can be dehydrated and rehydrated later if you so desire.

Taking the storage methods and potential shelf life should help you to choose what you'd get the most benefit from growing yourself. Make a list and note the time that it can be stored on a shelf or in the fridge. Add to your list if it can be pressure canned, frozen, or dehydrated.

Herbs in a Raised Bed

There are many herbs that can do well in raised bed gardens. In fact, some herbs need to be in a container, or they will take over your entire garden in a few seasons. Mint, for example, can spread rapidly. If you're looking to keep insects away, having it around is good, but not at the expense of choking out all other plant life.

Strategic placement of herbs is essential, and if you want to plant them in a raised bed, then some of them will need to be the only herb in the bed or find a way to divide your raised bed into sections so that they will not invade each other's space.

Many herbs need partials shade and won't enjoy being in the full sunshine all day long. It's best to consider finding a shadier place in the yard to set up a separate raised bed to grow these herbs in.

Herbs shouldn't be left out when you plant your garden each year because they are an integral part of cooking. You'll enjoy having fresh marjoram, tarragon, or cilantro to create specialties from your garden produce.

Herbs don't typically need any more care, or less, than other edibles such as vegetables or fruit. In fact, some herbs need very little help other than water at regular intervals. They can be considered invasive when planted straight into the ground, so raised beds are wonderfully suited for these types of plants.

Herbs that do well in raised beds:

In full sun:
- Mint
- Parsley
- Chives
- Cilantro
- Tarragon

Those that do best grown from planted seeds:
- Basil
- Borage
- Cilantro
- Dill
- Parsley
- Sage

Those that do best from cuttings from existing plants:
- Lavender
- Oregano
- Mint
- Sage
- Thyme

Those that need to be thinned and divided/transplanted:
- Bee balm
- Chives
- Garlic Chives

- Marjoram
- Oregano
- Thyme

How do you thin herbs?
One good way to thin your herb garden is to go through with a fork and use it at the roots to gently wiggle them apart from each other. Then carefully use the fork to lift the plant you wish to remove from below. Pull upward from loosened soil. Your soil should be very loose and well-drained as that is what herbs like the most. This will also make thinning easier.

You can transplant your thinned herbs to pots and sell them, give them as gifts, plant in other areas of your yard, or simply discard them if you've got nowhere left to plant them.

Herbs will continue to spread each season and you'll need to be prepared to thin them each season. Unlike many vegetables, most herbs grow back each season without the need to replant.

Many herbs are tender plants and don't do well in high winds and extreme weather conditions so you should consider planting them in places that they have some refuge from windy days and windy storms. If you've created a raised bed that has a removable cover, then this will allow you to cover them during inclement weather. Hail can ruin your garden.

How Do You Take a Cutting of a Plant/Herb?

Cuttings have been mentioned and it's important that if you are to have success with this method of cloning your plants, that you do so properly. You'll have the best success if you follow these simple directions.

1. Take only tender shoots off the main stem. Choose those that look healthy and are at least 3 to 6 inches in length. Cut the stem at an angle and just above a node for a leaf.

2. Remove the lower leaves on your cutting. Once you've got only stem near the bottom of your cutting, dip that end in growth hormone powder. This will be referred to as 'rooting powder', and you can find it in most garden stores.

3. Plant the powdered end of your shoot in a small 4-inch pot. You'll want to plant it approximately 2-inches deep. Ensure the soil is moist and kept moist. Cover your seedling in a plastic bag to create a miniature greenhouse that will stay warm and humid.

4. In approximately 2 weeks, check your plant for roots or new stems. Check them regularly during the first two weeks to ensure they are staying moist but not too wet. Water if necessary. If too moist, remove the bag and allow them to dry a bit. When roots and new stems or leaves are forming, you can transplant when ready.

*Basil, mint, and sage are so easy to grow from cuttings that they will grow roots in just a bowl of water.

Can They Come Inside Late in the Season?

Indeed, some herbs will enjoy coming inside and provide you with fresh herbs all winter long if you provide for their needs. A window with adequate sunshine, warmth, and water will keep these fresh herbs happy indoors:

- Basil
- Bay laurel
- Chives
- Mint
- Oregano
- Parsley
- Rosemary
- Thyme

Herbs are a wonderful starter plant for those who have never felt they had a green thumb. Most herbs don't attract insects because of their terpenes responsible for their flavor and aroma. Care is minimal and many will continue growing as long as you simply clip a few strands as you need them.

What Does Biennial, Perennial, and Annual Mean?

One of the things that you'll want to learn about plants is what type of plant they are. Aside from knowing what sort of fresh produce it provides to you, does it come back next year? Do you need to replant it each season? Will it have two crops in a year or when it is picked once is it done, like corn?

There are some things that you can plant that will come back year after year. There are also some things that won't produce for one or two seasons after you've planted it. Asparagus is often like this. Once you plant it, it may not produce anything you can eat until the following year.

So, what is each term and what plants are represented in each group? We cannot list every plant in existence, but each category is explained with the plants that are most popular within each of these categories.

Biennial - This is an example of a plant that takes two years to start and finish its life cycle. This plant will grow and flourish in the first season, survive the first winter, produce again in the next season, and then die.

Examples of Biennial plants
- Onions
- Leek
- Some members of the cabbage family
- Mullein (often considered a weed but can be eaten and cultivated)
- Parsley
- Fennel
- Silver beet
- Black-eyed Susan C
- Carrot

Perennial - This term is used for plants that live for more than two years. Most trees are considered perennials. It will have an undetermined life length. The main drawback of these is that it may take one to two seasons before they produce anything. The asparagus mentioned above is a perennial.

Examples of Perennial plants
- Raspberries, blueberries and most other berries
- Asparagus
- Rhubarb
- Kale
- Garlic
- Watercress

Annual - In one season, these plants grow from seed to flower, and produce a fruit or vegetable with seeds to carry on their species. Their life is over after they've fruited.

Examples of Annual plants:
- Watermelon
- Basil
- Corn
- Artichoke
- Arugula
- Carrots
- Chard
- Cilantro
- Cucumber
- Lettuce
- Peas
- Most pepper varieties

What Grows Well Together?

Some vegetables and fruits grow well together. This happens when some veggies give nutrition back to the soil for other plants to utilize, and therefore, they are a symbiotic relationship. This is most commonly called "companion planting". It's a great method for growth that doesn't require rows at all. Simply plant them together and allow them to be free-range plants in a raised bed.

The premise of companion planting is that one will provide a stem for another to climb on, while some perform the duties of ground cover, that keep the soil moist for longer and also strangle the growth of would-be weeds that don't get a chance to start growing. It is also related to plants that have complementary nutritional needs (e.g., one needs a lot of nitrogen but less potassium, the other the opposite).

One group of well-known companion plantings is nicknamed The Three Sisters. This refers to corn, squash, and a climbing bean. The corn should be planted approximately two weeks prior to the other two. The beans will use the corn to grow on while the squash will provide ground cover. Corn loves nutrition from the beans. This is why industrial farms will rotate between corn and soybeans each year. The beans give back what the corn depletes.

Companion planting also refers to using flowers in your gardens to naturally ward off insects. One of my favorite companion plants for vegetables (especially tomatoes) is marigolds. Marigolds ward off pests that threaten tomatoes, and I have beautiful spots of orange and yellow dotted around in my veggie garden.

Below is a list of companion plants. Adding this simple method to your gardening can have a powerful impact on the health and yield of your plants.

Asparagus loves - Basil, carrots, coriander, dill, marigolds, parsley, tomatoes.

Basil loves - Asparagus, beans, beets, bell peppers, cabbage, chili peppers, eggplant, marigolds, oregano, potatoes, tomatoes

Beans love - Beets, carrots, chard, cabbage, corn, cucumbers, peas, radishes.

Carrots love - Beans, lettuce, onions, peas, peppers, tomatoes

Potatoes love - Basil, beans, celery, corn, garlic, horseradish, lettuce, marigolds, onions, peas, radishes, spinach.

Strawberries love - Bush beans, caraway, chives, lettuce, onions, sage, spinach, squash.

Tomatoes love - Asparagus, carrots, celery, onions, parsley, peppers.

These are just a few examples of companion planting. You'll see some flowers mentioned. This is because they are known to deter bugs that are problematic for that particular vegetable. This helps you to garden and control pests naturally.

Pests are a natural problem with gardens -- you'll always have them. Using natural ways to deter them will help you grow organic, chemical-free food. Consider flowers around your raised beds, even if in separate pots.

You should also take heed that some plants don't like growing together and rather than love; they hate each other. Make sure that you read each packet of seeds carefully and when necessary, look elsewhere for answers. Google always has the advice to share on what plants need and don't like.

The square foot gardening method is essentially based on companion planting by using a square foot for one plant, another square foot for a different plant, and so on. You allow them to comingle and exist together in this way.

If you take your plant selection one step further and try to group them according to their needs for water, it will also make your gardening chores far easier when it comes to knowing how much water needs to go to your beds.

When choosing plants, ensure that you are planting them at the proper time and season. Some are better in fall, some are winter crops, while others should be started indoors in very early spring and then transplanted to the outdoors after the last frost has come and gone. (If you are working with a straw bale garden you can plant earlier in a cold climate.)

One key to knowing when to plant is to know your zone. The USDA provides a map so that you can determine the time to plant your vegetable garden.
https://planthardiness.ars.usda.gov/PHZMWeb/

The hardiness map will also know the temperature of your soil. Try using a thermometer in the soil as a guide to let you know when you can safely plant. Raised beds will warm sooner in the spring compared to the ground, straw bales can condition sooner and keep the plants warmer when there is a dip in spring temperatures.

This can be advantageous for those who live in cooler regions that have short growing seasons. You can even build a greenhouse or hoop house over your raised beds to prolong your growing season by several months each year. We have a big piece of folded plastic sheeting that is cut to size and ready in case we need to cover seedlings overnight when there is a cold snap in the spring.

Cold frames are like miniature greenhouses that are built over plants that are not cold-tolerant to get in one last crop before winter. These can be as simple as a small box with a window placed over the top, which can be removed as the weather is warmer. The fall can be unpredictable and cold frames simply help you to keep your plants protected and growing longer or started sooner in spring.

The use of "cloches" is like individual plants having their own tiny house. It is typical to remove them during the day as a plant may get burned or overheated, but they are very effective and easy for small gardens in that awkward transition time of winter to spring.[51] Consider staggering your plants so that things like lettuce - which is impossible to store for longer than about ten days - will always be ready to pick every two weeks, with a crop just the right size to last you for two weeks. This is the best utilization of your time and space.

As mentioned earlier, don't plant the things that will cast shadows closest to the sun. When you do this, you starve all the plants behind your corn of sunlight. It can't survive living in the shadow of your sweet corn. Plant your corn on the farthest end from the sun so that this situation doesn't happen to you.

Consider putting wheels under your raised bed frames so that you can move them or turn them as plants seem to be leaning or getting too much or not enough sunshine. This makes it easier for you to make some adjustments to ensure that your plants are getting ideal sunlight

Choosing Your Seeds

One common mistake that is made by new gardeners is that they choose cheap seeds, from unknown sources, without any knowledge of the plants these seeds came from. In other words, plants that are not labeled as organic or heirloom have very likely been sourced from plants that were grown using chemical pesticides and fertilizers.

These seeds may also be very old, which will greatly impact their viability. In other words, they may not sprout. The main argument for organic seed is that you are supporting organic farmers when you use them. You're helping farmers who work hard to be kind to the earth and produce food crops that are free of harmful chemicals. By selling their seed, they are creating an additional flow of income and sharing their bounty with you far beyond being able to purchase their fresh produce.

Heirloom or Organic?
Organic means that the seed has come from produce that was grown in soil that was free of chemical additives and was not sprayed with pesticides that could be harmful to the earth. You're supporting organic farmers, and that's great, but what is an heirloom seed? Why would you want those and who does that support? What is the difference?

Heirloom speaks more to the heritage of a particular plant species. Heirloom seeds are from openly pollinated plants that pass on their characteristics to their offspring, via the seeds. Just because a plant is an heirloom variety does not mean that it is also organic. It can be organic or not. Read the package carefully to see if it says organic on the label. If it doesn't say it is organic, then it is not.

How Long Do Seeds Keep?
You can safely keep seeds for as long as 2 years without concern. Some seeds will keep for as long as 5 years, but the problem is that you don't know how long they have been sitting in a warehouse when you buy them, especially with large chains and discount stores that may be buying stock years ahead to get a good price.

The key is to try to get seeds that are under 2-years-old. Then, if you don't plant them all the first year or two that you've got them, you can be relatively certain that they'll still be viable.

Best Places to Buy Seeds?
There are many places that specialize in organic seeds. A little research will yield a ton of results for you to choose from. Consider a co-op or an organic business close to you. Some seed exchanges also exist locally, and you can join them, like a club. Each year, they happily swap seeds with each other to share variety and learn best practices for each variety. Each gardener has their own unique style, technique, and growing medium (soil).

Sometimes you can gather seeds from friends and neighbors who share with you as well. Seeds are lightweight and easy to mail to others. Making holiday gifts that are filled with seeds to plant the following spring is a great way to exchange your seeds with family.

Collecting your own seeds?

Some gardeners find that they enjoy a particular tomato or cucumber so much that keeping some seeds seems like a great idea ... and it is. Not all plants go to seed and allow you to easily save some. Carrots, for example (remember our list of biennials), need to be left in the ground for a second year in order to go to seed.

In order to gather your own seeds, make sure that you use clean, sterilized utensils. You'll want a sharp knife, some scissors, clean paper packets that you can label easily, and that is all.

You'll need to learn when the best time to collect your seeds is. Late in the season is best and some seeds will come from your fruits and veggies directly. Squash seeds are not recommended to be saved as they rarely grow the following year. There are some vegetables that you can easily save seed from and they are wonderful ones to start with.

Easy produce to harvest seeds from:
- Tomatoes
- Peppers
- Beans
- Peas

The above plants are self-pollinating and are easy to produce year after year by collecting your own seed. Other plants, such as cucumbers or squash, are far more difficult because they have both male and female plants that pollinate each other. This can produce offspring that are hybrids and not the same as the produce your garden grew the year before.

Make sure that you've saved seeds from those that were labeled as 'open-pollinated' so that they continue to reproduce with the same lineage of produce. Seeds labeled F1 are more often those raised in large commercial operations and are hybrids. This will be difficult for you to grow. This makes another case for growing heirloom seeds to start with and why so many people lean toward them.

When you gather your seeds, you'll want to save them and label them with the name/variety/ and the date they were bagged. Some seeds are hard to gather, such as tomato seeds. They will be difficult to separate from the fluid inside the fruit. Drop them into a jar of water and allow them to soak a few days until the seeds come loose and fall to the bottom of the far.

You may then dry them. They should be fully dry before placing them into your paper envelope that is properly labeled with their name, variety, and date. Store them in a dark, cool, and dry location in your home.

Pepper seeds should be taken from fruits that you allow to stay on the vine until they begin to wrinkle slightly. The seeds are easy to separate. Allow them to dry and then store in your paper envelopes.

With both peas and beans, leave them on the vine until the shells turn brown. Pick them and allow them to dry in the shell for two weeks. When they are dry, shell them and store the seeds as you have the others. You can also leave them in the pods until you are ready to plant the seeds the following year if you desire. It will not hurt them in any way to remain in the dried pods.

Reading Seed Packets

Surprisingly, the seed packets contain virtually all of the information that you need to be successful in growing your plants if you pay attention. It is surprising how many people don't even glance at the package. This is sad because there is a great deal of information on the packet for you to read.

Seed packets all contain the same basic information. It will contain the seed lot number, the sell-by date, the country of origin, and the name of the seed company.

Your seeds will be labeled as to whether they are organic or heirloom if they are of either variety. The common name and the scientific name will be on the packet in most cases. This can help you to look up further information if you so desire. For example, Cucumber, White Spine, Cucumis sativus. This tells us that this is a cucumber. The variety is called White Spine, and the scientific name is Cucumis sativus.

There will be a description on the back of the packet that will tell you if this is disease or rot-resistant, what special things you should know about it, and in the case of this cucumber, the label reads,

*"Excellent disease-resistant, vigorous plants. Medium green with small white spines. Internal structure solid and crisp. Bears many small, blocky fruits with tender skins. This variety is perfect for making all types of pickles. **Culture**: Plant in groups of 6-8 seeds, 4-5 feet between groups. Thin to 3-4 seedlings per group. **Harvest**: 1 ½" long for tiny sweets to 5"-6" long for robust dills and spears. Frequent picking promotes more blossoms. **Yields**: Extremely well.*

Uses: *May use in fresh salads but this variety was bred for making pickles."*

Not only does this label tell you all that you need to know to plant these seeds, thin them and use the fruits of your labor, there is also a chart below that which shows you what depth to plant the seeds, how far apart to space them, how many days to germinate the seeds, and how many days to maturity (when you should be able to expect to pick them). Some seed packets will also have the hardiness zones on the back of the packets to show you when to plant this particular seed.

This means that if you keep your labels, you'll always know what is going on with your plants. You will know *when* to plant, *how* to plant, how to *care* for them, and *even when they should be ready to harvest*. One very good way to label your garden and have the information at your fingertips at all times is to make a copy of the back of the seed packet, which has all the information, add the date you planted the seeds, cover it with a Ziplock bag to keep it safe from weather and staple it to a stick in the soil next to your plants.

Labeling Plants is Critical: Why?

If you don't know what it is, then you won't know when it is ready, how should you thin seedlings appropriately, and when to harvest your produce at its peak. Always label your plants and keep track of your garden.

Plant Your Seedlings

When you decide what to grow, where to place your beds, and have your soil all in place, it's a matter of starting your plants in the best way to give them the best start in your garden. There are some plants that should be started indoors so that they can be transplanted outside as soon as the weather is warm enough.

Plants that should be started indoors include; tomatoes, peppers, beets, cabbage, celery, cucumbers, and many types of lettuce. Start them indoors 6 to 10 weeks prior to your last expected frost. Once you are in the clear of frost, you can begin taking your seedlings outside for a few hours each day in the warm weather.

When spacing your plant seeds, refer to the packaging and understand that you'll likely have to pull some excess when all the seeds sprout. You should plant on some seeds not germinating. It happens. Sometimes old seeds won't germinate, and sometimes they just aren't hardy seeds, to begin with.

When you pull your excess, you can transplant them to small pots and continue to grow them, give them away, sell them, or plant them elsewhere. When simply culling, make sure to choose the best-looking young sprouts to be left from your thinning work.

Allowing them to gradually grow accustomed to the outdoor climate and humidity levels by slowly increasing the amount of time they are outdoors prior to transplanting them will ensure they are healthy and hardy once in your soil. This process is referred to as hardening off.

There are other vegetables that do best when they are planted directly into the soil where they will be grown. Corn is just such a type of plant. It does best when seeded where it will grow. Others include carrots, radishes, and most other root vegetables.

Some people will have a fan blowing very gently on their indoor seedlings. This forces the stem to grow stronger, giving the young plant more endurance for outdoor weather later on. If you don't have a nice sunny area for your seedlings, consider using a UVB light that will provide them with artificial sunlight that will help them thrive and reach for the sky as they grow.

When you transplant your seedlings, take special care to gently remove them from their plastic containers by rolling them in your hands as you softly squeeze. Tip them until they slide out easily. Place them into a hole large enough to accommodate the entire pot of soil. Use your fingers to very softly loosen the root ball so that the roots will relax in the new spacious soil.

Pull soil up around them and pat it down firmly around their base but do not pack it tightly. Consider using some mulch to hold the moisture at their base, so you can water less frequently. Then water them at their base, thoroughly wetting the mulch.

Going forward, only water them at their base and do not water your plants at midday. They should be watered early in the morning and late in the evening, without getting their tender leaves wet. Wet leaves will fry in the blistering sunshine of summer and kill them.

Ensure that your soil remains damp but isn't holding water to the point of being slurry. Roots must be in damp soil but not sit in water. If the roots remain too wet, they'll begin to rot. You can check for root rot, if you suspect it, by removing the root of one plant and examining it. A healthy root should be white and free of parasites or mold. It should feel firm and crisp, rather than soft and gray in color. Gray roots are an indication of root rot.

Using Technology to Help You Garden

This is an excellent way to set yourself up for success. You've got some choices in the technology that you use, but it's wonderful once you try a few ways and decide what feels right for you. There are gardening apps that will help you plan your garden, recommend which things will grow best next to each other, and help you track the time until they are ready to harvest, based on when you plant.

Some really great apps will prompt you to water your plants, check them regularly and tell you what to check, or even help you diagnose problems such as mold when you spot them. Imagine having an app that lets you snap a photo of a bug or leaf damage, and it tells you what caused the damage and how to rectify it. This makes gardening so much more accessible to those who have never had a garden or find that it has been so many years that they truly don't remember much.

You can also use Google Calendar to simply set reminders to tell you when you should check your garden and actually 'schedule it' in your day. You can even have the calendar set to sound an alarm that tells you it is time to harvest your green beans. Take advantage of any type of technology that you can think of that may help you.

Maintaining and Troubleshooting Your Garden

Diagnosing Parasite Issues

Some plants are often prone to parasite issues. Corn will fall victim to corn borers, or corn worms, that can be found at the tip of each new ear of corn when you peel back the leaves. Organically grown corn is likely to have one and generally, the top of the ear can simply be snapped off, cornworm and all. Wash the ears well, and they're still fine.

To avoid hornworms naturally, you may spray beneficial nematodes directly on the silks to control the worms. You can also dust the plants with a product called Safer Garden Dust and repeat the dustings weekly until the corn silks turn brown. At this point, it should be safe from the cornworm.

There are horned caterpillars that invade tomato plants. They are very large caterpillars that can be the size of your thumb. They may be called a tomato worm, a horned worm, a horned caterpillar, and they don't always attack tomato plants. These 'worms' will also feast on your peppers, eggplants, and potatoes.

When they do attack your tomatoes, they will eat tomato plants by chewing large holes in the leaves. They can and will kill your plants if left to eat unchecked. You can rid your plants of them by physically removing and killing them. They aren't easily killed by any sprays. Some birds will prey upon them but the best way to control them is to physically pull them off the plants and drop them into something that kills them.

They are green, camouflage as leaves, and they hide very well. For this reason, they are nearly impossible to spot during the day when they are hidden. Take a flashlight and go out after dark to find them. They'll be out in the open, munching on your plants. The best way to dispose of them that is the least offensive is to drop them into a bucket of soapy water in which they will drown. Later, toss that into your compost pile (as long as the soap is castile soap or other natural soap that is free of chemicals).

Cabbage moths, another destructive garden pest, will hover around your plants and eat holes in your cabbage plants and other leafy greens. To keep them away naturally, plant cabbage near tomatoes. The moths hate tomato plants and don't typically go anywhere near them. You can also plant marigolds and thyme near your cabbage and they naturally deter the cabbage month.

Aphids in the garden are also quite common. They are one of the bugs that can be a nightmare to the gardener's life. The best way to naturally control them is to spray them with vinegar and water. A spray bottle with ⅔ water and ⅓ white vinegar can be sprayed directly on plants and will kill aphids and their eggs on contact.

If you choose a living insect killer, like the praying mantis, you'll need to be sure that you don't use anything that can harm them. They are typically ordered in a pod that you keep in a jar until it hatches out and you'll have hundreds of babies at that time. Turn them loose in the garden and watch them do their work. It's a wonderful project to involve children in as they do require a bit of care and size before you can release them into your garden, where they'll grow fat and happy on the bugs that come around, including aphids.

Remember that when you use natural remedies, they often need to be reapplied. Some things need to be sprayed daily. Diatomaceous Earth has to be reapplied after each rain. These products are not expensive and will ensure that your food is always free of chemicals that will leech into the soil and contaminate groundwater. When synthetic chemicals are used, they differ from natural molecules.

A natural compound is created when molecules are attracted to each other and bind together. Oxygen is an example of this type of compound. It is easily changed to carbon dioxide, which is then used by plantlife, who create, through the process of photosynthesis, oxygen again.

Synthetic chemicals are sadly manufactured and created in such a way that they do not ever breakdown. They don't lose or gain molecules to become anything else. This means that they don't biodegrade and in their constant state, may do harm to the environment. When a synthetically produced molecule, such as that in a chemical insecticide or fertilizer enters the food cycle, the soil, and the water supply, it eventually finds its way into your body, where it remains.

No one knows precisely what synthetics can do to the human body, but it's a fair conclusion that this may be the cause of cancers rising in large numbers across the world, particularly in places where there is a high use of these sorts of chemicals. In fact, large lawsuits have been won, with the courts feeling there is enough evidence to prove both cancer and birth defects, along with other chronic conditions being the aftermath of long-term exposure to these chemicals. This is the reason we've stuck to natural gardening methods here and highly recommend that you learn them as well.

Common Natural Garden Alternatives and Solutions

When it comes to garden pests, you're going to have them. Prepare yourself mentally because each time you plant a garden, you are ringing a dinner bell for parasites of all sorts.

In the interest of helping you do things as naturally as possible; this section is to give you some alternative methods to keep your plants healthy and insect-free. There are many time-tested methods for raising healthy plants that go back to our ancient ancestors who were successful gardeners long before herbicides and chemical pesticides.

Had they not been successful, we would not be here. Also, many of our fruits and vegetables wouldn't be here either. There are ways to be successful and beat the bugs this year. Read on for suggestions.

Garlic Tea

Garlic tea is a good solution that can be sprayed to prevent insects. They do not like the smell or taste. It needs to be reapplied frequently throughout the season but works very well for many types of moths, worms, and flying insects.

To make garlic tea:
In a blender, thoroughly liquify 2 to 3 bulbs of fresh garlic. Add 1 and 1/2 cups of water. Strain it so you can spray it without clogs. Add any additional water to fill a gallon container and use it immediately. You can freeze it as well but don't keep it more than a day or two at room temperature as it will wreak. You will quickly understand why insects won't come near it.

Seaweed Fertilizer

Seaweed is rich in nutrients. It is excellent for gardens and improves any soil. You can use dried, ground seaweed and spread it directly on the ground around plants. You can also soak seaweed in water to create a tea from it and pour it at the base of plants. You should soak it for at least two weeks to get all the nutrients from the seaweed into the water.

Habanero Insecticide

Chop and grind a handful of hot peppers in a blender. Roughly 10 cayenne peppers are best but use what you have, as long as they are hot peppers. Add a gallon of water while it is in the blender (or as much as you can fit). Then strain this through a wire screen and add more water if you need to so that you've got a full gallon. Pour this into a spray bottle and use it where you have an insect problem.

Please, be careful when doing this. Wear eye protection and leave the lid on the blender after you shut it off and allow things to settle before pouring. This method is best done with no children or pets around, and gloves should be worn. Do not touch your face after touching hot peppers.

Used Coffee Grounds

They can be added to soil to improve the aeration, moisture retention, and attract natural earthworms to your soil. They provide food to microorganisms living in the soil to make it a thriving place for nutrients and plants to root in. Simply save your grounds after each pot. Dump them onto paper towel or newspaper and allow them to dry and then add them to your garden or your compost pile for next year's garden. It's a great way to recycle your waste and put it to good use right away.

Spray for Mildew and Brown or Black Spots

This mildew is a common problem in some gardens. Humid environments make it more probable that you'll experience it at one time or another. A simple fix is to create a spray that changes the pH to make mold unable to flourish. Do not spray it directly onto the soil. You can change the pH of your soil, which you do not want. This spray should be sprayed directly onto the spots on the plant, in a fine mist.

4 Tbsp baking soda
1 tsp baby soap or mild soap
1 gallon of water

Mix these into any garden spray jug or pour into a spray bottle as needed. You can store this indefinitely. It won't go bad and it will not stink.

Aluminum Stalk Shields
Wrapping the stems of plants that are prone to cutworms will protect them from damage. This will work for tomatoes that are the favorite food of the horned worm. They will eat stems and leaves until the plants are decimated.

Eggshells
Keep your empty eggshells, wash them, dry them, and crush them. These can be planted with tomato plants to provide additional nutrients to the soil for tomatoes. Eggshells will also rid your garden of snails and slugs as they can't move over the sharp shells.

Caring for Your Garden

When you plant your garden, you'll need to check it regularly. The plants that are growing within the soil can begin to deplete the soil of nutrients. You should check your pH and your soil every 10 to 14 days to ensure that your garden still has what it needs to continue to grow strong and healthy.

What is Photosynthesis?

Plant life uses photosynthesis to create their food from sunshine, carbon dioxide, and water - all of which are readily available in the atmosphere around them. The by-product of this act we call photosynthesis is that the carbon dioxide molecule is changed in composition to become an oxygen molecule, which mammals use to provide us with the air we breathe that keeps us alive.

Watering

Watering your garden needs to be done in the morning before the sun has risen to the heat of the day. The earlier you water, the better. You should strive for your leaves to have no sun on them when the sunlight begins to heat them, you run the chance of burning holes and brown spots into your leaves and this can kill the plant by reducing the ability of the leaves to photosynthesize, an important process to your plant's growth.

The caveat with watering standard raised beds is that they are above the ground and contain a relatively small amount of earth that will warm more rapidly than the ground. This means that they dry faster and may require more water to keep the soil moist enough to provide the proper environment for your plants. The contained space also means that you may need to ensure that there is enough drainage.) You'll need to check regularly for damp soil that is preferred over dry or wet soil.

If you are using straw bales or hügelkultur as your raised beds, then you have both moisture retention as well as better drainage making watering an easier task.

Determining how much water your garden needs isn't difficult, it just takes observation and experience. You can use a moisture thermometer[52] by inserting it 2" deep, or just test it with your fingers – if it's dry at that depth then water, if not, then skip that day.

You can always run a permanent water line to mist your plants at regular intervals. If you build this system yourself, it's not overly expensive. You can also lay down a soaker hose in your beds and water at intervals set by a timer.

I don't like sprinklers in my raised bed, or any veggie or flower garden, for that matter. The spray wastes water and it is not a method for soaking deeply. The result is that the roots of your plants are shallower and not as stable. Also, sprinklers leave water all over the leaves, so that your plants may be in danger of burning if the sun comes out before the water is dry. It can also promote mold.

The soaker hose method is excellent because it places the water at the roots where it is needed, slowly being released so that it doesn't wash nutrients from the soil or get the leaves wet. The water goes deep down where the roots need it.

There are a number of companies who make drip irrigation systems. They have the advantages of a soaker hose, plus you can customize the water release to each different plant. The downside is that they take time and focus to set up. Drip systems are more expensive to set up, but last longer. You can expect to replace soaker hoses every one or two years.

Leaves can wither in the sun if not fully dry by the time the sunshine is on them directly. Sunshine is magnified by the water droplets and can scorch tender leaves, leaving them burned, withered, and damaged. When the leaves are damaged from scorching, they cannot photosynthesize as needed and it will kill the plant.

My preference is a soaker hose or drip system on a timer. My vegetable garden is well watered before I get up.

Adding mulch on top of your soil does three main things:
1) Mulch helps retain moisture, especially in the hottest summer months.
2) It also helps keep a constant friendly temperature for the roots.
3) It keeps weeds at bay.

You can purchase mulch from a garden center or put about 4" of dry leaves or straw on top of the soil around your plants.

I live in a place that regular, sunny days in the 90'sF. I find mulch very useful in my raised bed gardens around the house, but I've never felt the need to use mulch with the straw bales that hold the vegetable garden.

Winterizing Your Garden

Quite often, we harvest our bounty of fresh food from our gardens and get busy with the storage of that harvest. We forget the importance of winterizing our garden for the following spring. Why do we need to do this? Simply because it will give your garden the boost and readiness required to plant early the following season, knowing that your plants will already have nutrients available.

Taking some steps after you harvest and before winter will help to keep your garden healthy. Taking advantage of the composting and breaking down of the remnants of your garden over the winter will result in rich soil the following spring. In fact, taking care to winterize your garden can help you grow some crops right through the winter.

The very first thing that you should know, in order to know when to winterize your garden is to know what zone you're living in. This will tell you when you are likely to experience your season's first frost of the winter and when the last frost is most likely to occur in spring. The USDA website has all of this information, as well as other important articles that you may find very helpful.

Steps in winterizing your garden:

1. Begin cutting back and pruning the plants that have produced their crop and will grow again next year. This will include your berries, grapes, and so forth. Clip them back and add the trimmings to your compost pile.

2. Weed. This is the time to remove all of your weeds and invasive plants that you don't want in your garden. Compost these separately or burn them so that you don't accidentally add weed seeds to your compost that can infest your garden the following year. Also, remove any pieces of vegetables or fruits that may be on the ground to ensure that you don't have volunteers the following year.

3. Now is the time to divide your perennials. They should be separated and replanted at least 6 weeks prior to the anticipation of the first freeze. This being because you want them to have the opportunity to be fully rooted and settled into place before the first freeze.

4. Now is the time to add compost as much as 3 to 4 inches thick on top of your garden beds. If you need to remove some dirt from your raised bed gardens, you may remove that soil and then transfer it to your compost pile where it will be rejuvenated by spring next season.

5. Mulch in places where you've got beds on the ground, your walkways and anywhere else necessary. These things are best done in the fall so that you don't have to do them in the spring when it can be muddy, and you are absorbed with getting your garden started with new plants.

Proper harvesting techniques

The vast majority of plants are easy to harvest simply by twisting and pulling the vegetables. With corn, you may use one hand to support the stalk while you pull and twist the ear of corn in a downward motion to pull it from the stalk.

Tomatoes can be twisted from the vines. If they are fully ripe, they'll pull free very easily. The same is true for cucumbers, beans, and peas. If necessary, use a small pair of garden nippers, like scissors, in your gardening apron. You can use that to quickly cut your produce free without any concern about harming the main plant stalk.

Always remember to support the stalk when you remove plants from it, so that it doesn't snap or bend under the force. For root vegetables, they are easily grasped low on the stem, just above the ground, and slowly pulled straight upward. Radishes, onions, and carrots will be harvested in this manner.

Root vegetables are best when harvested at the point in which the top of the root vegetable is just visible at the surface of the soil. This will typically tell you that they are fully grown and ready when ripe. Refer to your seed pack to ensure that it has been long enough. Pull one and if necessary, you can wait on the rest another few days.

Conclusion

Raised bed gardens are one of the most versatile and creative ways in which you can choose to grow your vegetables. Providing food for your family is the primary goal, but you'll also find that it is a fantastic hobby to get you outdoors and enjoying the fresh air. It is a learning experience for your entire family.

It's a project that starts with planning, then building, and finally planting. Be careful because gardening is typically addictive to most people. Don't expect to pick strawberries with small children who are tall enough to reach them, because most berries are enjoyed outside in the sunshine, fresh from the plant.

There is nothing that tastes as good as a vine-ripe tomato, and when you taste the difference between your tomatoes and the store's hothouse ones, you'll never want to buy produce ever again. Most people expand their garden after the first season. Many people grow more than they need and give food to neighbors. There really is no such thing as too much food from the garden. Share it!

If your neighbors are going to plant a garden each year as well, why not get together with them and make sure you aren't growing the same things? Grow enough to swap some with them so you both have more variety without more expense and work. A lot of neighborhoods practice this sort of vegetable sharing type of gardening.

Some neighborhoods even have community gardens where you can volunteer and in return, receive a portion of the crop each year. This is a wonderful way to learn gardening. There will always be others who are willing to help you. Growing a garden makes you a member of an elite group of people who have returned to their roots and taken feeding their family back into their own hands.

Gardening has also been proven to lower blood pressure and help improve cognitive function. It's wonderful for reducing anxiety as well. When we age, our hands develop arthritis and grow weaker. Gardening can help strengthen them.

Cardiovascular health is improved with any form of exercise and gardening is surely a great deal of exercise. You'll find muscles that you didn't know even existed. Don't forget to stretch and take the time to clear your head as well. Gardening can help make you happy.

The additional sunshine helps your body to process Vitamin D, which plays an important role in moods and reducing depression. Many people suffer from Seasonal Affective Disorder in the months that they can't get outside and in Alaska where daylight wanes in winter. No worries about that during the gardening season.

Lastly, you will enjoy extra sleep that you get from being more tired. When you spend time outdoors in the sunshine, you'll tend to sleep more soundly and have fewer problems with falling asleep at night. When you do fall asleep, you'll sleep more deeply for longer as well.

Aside from the health benefits, you will be saving money. The average family with a small garden saves as much as $500 per year on their groceries. The larger the garden, the more the savings.

Your initial start-up costs will set you back in the first season, but if you pay attention to the materials, we recommended that your raised beds will last you for many seasons. Raised beds are a wonderful tool that you can use for years that will help you provide hundreds of pounds of food for your household.

This means that with each year that goes by, the more of your costs you recuperate and save. Put that money toward paying something else off or enjoying time with your family the rest of the year, doing more with them.

As you can see, raised bed gardening can easily be modified and adapted to suit your needs and growing seasons, making it one of the most versatile methods of gardening that you can utilize.

Remember that you don't have to choose one! I live with a straw bale vegetable garden, planters for herbs outside my door, a hügelkultur and 3" raised beds wrapped around my house on two sides. I am planning to construct an herb spiral in the next year.

You give a lot to your garden, but you receive back tenfold. Your outlook on life is likely to be improved as you save money and feel better. You'll live longer, and your kids will grow-up feeling satisfaction in helping to build something and watch it produce plants that thrive. One of the greatest gifts you can give to your kids and grandkids is to teach them how to grow their own food.

Appendix
Instructions for a Basic 4X4 Raised Bed

If you are using any type of wood or material that will require screws, nails, or hardware, spend a little extra for stainless steel. It won't rust and it won't eventually break down and release anything toxic or just rust until it falls out.

If you plan on painting your wood beds, don't paint the inside unless you know you are using a non-toxic, biodegradable paint that won't off-gas. That's the only way you can be sure that nothing finds its way into your food.

It's worth noting that some people will add a liner of some sort. Again, beware that many types of plastic liners will leach toxic BPAs into your soil, and you would be better off to have no liner at all. Just plain wood is more organic and certainly safer in the end.

To put together a basic raised bed made of wood, the simplest way is to use 2x4s for corner posts. For the sideboards, you'll want a 1 inch by 4 inches by whatever depth you want. You can get boards in widths up to 20 inches wide, which is plenty deep for any raised bed.

Use a corner square to ensure that you are making 90-degree angles. By using a 2x4 in each corner, you'll have something solid and already square to attach your board to, so keeping things nicely square will be easier.

Raised beds don't need a bottom if you are placing them directly on the ground. You will want to lay down several layers of newspaper or weed barrier before adding your soil. If you've got any burrowing animals, or aren't sure if you do, then you should also put down a layer of hardware cloth. This will prevent gophers and moles from digging into your bed from below.

Beds that are lifted to a higher level for your ease of access will require a bottom. Your choices for this are the same as above and wood is again the best option when you can get it. You can use a sheet of plywood, but it will eventually rot, even if pressure treated. Cedar would be ideal. Don't forget that you'll need to add plenty of drain holes so that your raised bed has enough drainage to prevent your roots from rotting in water.

It's very easy to overwater things and when soil isn't given a proper way to adequately drain, the roots will rot, and mold can also grow. This can create situations where plants simply wither and die. They may be fine and suddenly begin turning yellow and begin to wilt. This is usually the result of having wet roots.

When you don't drill enough drainage holes into the base of your beds, you'll run the risk of overwatering plants and killing them before they've had a chance to grow. Proper drainage is one of the most critical elements of proper soil and growing hearty, healthy plants.

If you want your beds to be 4 feet wide and 4 feet long, you should cut your sides to 48 inches in length and the two ends should be 46 inches (because the 1 inch of thickness from the sides will make it a total of 48 inches).

Your bottom or base will be 48 inches wide and 48 inches long. This is considered one of the best sizes for reaching all parts of the bed, all the way around. Always work on a level surface so you keep your frame level and square as you work.

If you're a carpenter extraordinaire, by all means, design your own beds in shapes and sizes that fit your needs and be as creative as you like. There's really no wrong way to do it if it works for you. As long as it drains efficiently and you can reach everything, you're good to go.

FOOTNOTES

1
https://www.ippc.int/en/

https://en.wikipedia.org/wiki/IPPC

https://www.instructables.com/id/How-to-determine-if-a-wood-pallet-is-safe-for-use/

https://www.thebalancesmb.com/are-wood-pallets-safe-for-crafting-misinformation-abounds-2878158

https://www.1001pallets.com/pallet-safety/

[3] https://www.youtube.com/watch?v=anL1KG_u4NM

[4] https://www.familyhandyman.com/garden-structures/how-to-build-raised-garden-beds/

[5] https://www.instructables.com/id/Reclaimed-Wood-Raised-Bed-Garden/

[6] https://www.instructables.com/id/Raised-Garden-Beds-and-More-from-Reclaimed-Wood/

[7] https://queenbeecoupons.com/and-so-we-grow-building-raised-beds-for-the-first-time-about-35-each/

[8] https://www.goodhousekeeping.com/home/gardening/g20706096/how-to-build-a-simple-raised-bed/

[9] https://eartheasy.com/cedar-complete-raised-garden-bed-kit-8-x-12/?sku=RB812&msclkid=314a787cf56211fe989c26ae2f1a8b8e&utm_source=

bing&utm_medium=cpc&utm_campaign=NCA%3A%20Shopping%3A%20Non-Branded%3A%201a.%20General%20%3E%20Raised%20Garden%20Beds%3A%20USA&utm_term=4583863987366385&utm_content=Shopping%20(product)%3A%201.%20General%3A%20Yard%20%26%20Garden%20%3E%20Raised%20Garden%20Beds

[10] https://www.goodshomedesign.com/learn-how-to-build-a-u-shaped-raised-garden-bed/

[11] https://brittanystager.com/how-to-build-a-u-shaped-raised-garden-bed-drawing-and-rendering/

[12] https://en.wikipedia.org/wiki/Keyhole_garden

[13] https://en.wikipedia.org/wiki/Keyhole_garden

[14] https://permaculturefoodforest.wordpress.com/2016/04/14/keyhole-gardens/

[15] https://permaculturefoodforest.wordpress.com/2016/04/14/keyhole-gardens/

[16] https://permaculturefoodforest.wordpress.com/2016/04/14/keyhole-gardens/

[17] https://www.ruralsprout.com/trellis-squash/

[18] https://growsomethinggreen.com/blogs/grow-something-green/squash-and-gourd-tunnels-that-will-simply-amaze-you

[19] Video guides to building squash archs
https://www.youtube.com/watch?v=Vy35ABY6weA

https://www.youtube.com/watch?v=r4PVafxurf4
https://www.youtube.com/watch?v=UND6488kBJk
https://www.atlantagardeningforum.com/growing-winter-squash-up-a-trellis-update-5-24-2012/

[20] https://pondinformer.com/pond-fish-that-eat-mosquito-larvae/

https://www.sandiegocounty.gov/content/sdc/deh/pests/wnv/prevention/chd_wnv_mosquito_fish.html#:~:text=Mosquitofish%20are%20small%20freshwater%20fish,swimming%20pools%2C%20fountains%20and%20ponds.

[21] https://www.nytimes.com/2013/03/21/garden/grasping-at-straw-a-foolproof-vegetable-plot.html?smid=fb-share&_r=0

[22] https://strawbalegardens.com/photos/before-after-2/

[23] Average size of a large bag of organic potting soil is 45.5 lbs
https://www.lowes.com/pd/FoxFarm-Foxfarm-FX14047-Happy-Frog-Ph-Adjusted-Garden-Potting-Soil-Mix-2-cu-ft/1002825800

Here is a blood meal example:
https://www.lowes.com/pd/Jobe-s-Organics-Blood-Meal-Plant-Food-3-lb-Natural-All-Purpose-Food/50040766

Here is one organic liquid plant food.
https://www.arbico-organics.com/product/2618/seaweed-kelp-fertilizers-for-cannabis?gclid=CjOKCQjwlN32BRCCARIsADZ-J4vNqYKH8XNj4ftLQrhb59AuTHxr1vmGd02r0ZwhSIlpdBfXS8xsnuEaAjzLEALw_wcB

[24] https://www.amazon.com/Support-Upgrade-Trellis-Climbing-Watering/dp/B08732ZKMM/ref=asc_df_B08732ZKMM/?tag=bingshoppinga-20&linkCode=df0&hvadid=&hvpos=&hvnetw=o&hvrand=&hvpone=&hvptwo=&hvqmt=e&hvdev=c&hvdvcmdl=&hvlocint=&hvlocphy=&hvtargid=pla-4583795268946187&psc=1

[25] https://joegardener.com/podcast/gardening-in-straw-bales/

[26] This thermometer has a 20" stem so you can accurately gauge what's happening in your straw bale conditioning process: https://www.amazon.com/REOTEMP-Backyard-Compost-Thermometer-Instructions/dp/B002P5RGMI/ref=sr_1_2?dchild=1&keywords=compost+thermometer&qid=1591201568&sr=8-2

[27] Straw Bale Gardens Complete: Updated Kindle Edition by Joel Karsten. Cool Springs Press: P. 79

[28] Herrman Andrä used the term Hugelkultur in a gardening booklet. https://en.wikipedia.org/wiki/H%C3%BCgelkultur

[29] Hugelkultur

Benefits: https://morningchores.com/hugelkultur/

[30] https://morningchores.com/hugelkultur/
https://www.gardening-advice.net/hugelkultur.html

[31] https://www.fascinatewithzea.com/hugelkultur-spiral-garden/

[32] Soil stability analysis: https://en.wikipedia.org/wiki/Slope_stability_analysis

[33] This site gives you more detail about hugelkultur and illustrates more options for configuring your mound. https://richsoil.com/hugelkultur

[34] Critical questions about hugelkultur:
https://www.gardenmyths.com/hugelkultur-gardening-hugelkultur-raised-beds/

[35] https://www.gardeningchannel.com/how-to-build-an-herb-spiral/
https://gardenandhappy.com/herb-spiral/

[36] https://lifestyle.photomontages.club/landscaping/herbal-spiral-build-yourself-great-pictures-and-building-instructions/

[37] Another simple tomato cage tutorial – 4 steps, printable, not a video.
https://www.diynetwork.com/how-to/outdoors/gardening/how-to-make-a-wire-tomato-cage

This site shows another way to use metal livestock panel as a support, the material list estimates the cost to be about $2/per tomato plant
https://www.motherearthnews.com/diy/garden-yard/tomato-cages-zm0z11zphe#ArticleContent

The same site shows the idea of using or building a ladder that can then be easily folded for storage during the winter
https://www.motherearthnews.com/diy/garden-yard/tomato-cages-zm0z11zphe#ArticleContent

Here are 10 "cheap and easy" tomato cages including a beautiful bamboo example.
https://www.gardenersmag.com/10-cheap-and-easy-diy-tomato-cages/

[38] Trellis instructions and ideas
https://georgiapellegrini.com/2018/08/27/blog/pioneer-skills/how-to-trellis-your-raised-bed-garden/
Simple frame and string trellis for raised beds
https://www.finegardening.com/article/diy-raised-bed-trellis
Another frame and string or fishing wire trellis instruction
https://www.youtube.com/watch?v=gH3-5VXWpZQ

[39] https://morningchores.com/raised-garden-bed-plans/2/

[40] https://www.lowes.com/pl/Landscape-fabric-Landscape-fabric-stakes-Landscaping-Outdoors/4294612873

[41] https://www.lowes.com/search?searchTerm=plastic+sheeting

[42] https://www.lowes.com/search?searchTerm=bird+netting

[43] https://www.thesun.co.uk/archives/news/1031475/robin-williams-15-funniest-stand-up-jokes-and-routines/

[44] https://www.redbrand.com/deer-orchard-wildlife-fence/

[45] https://iamcountryside.com/fences-sheds-barns/deer-fencing-tips-protect-wildlife-and-gardens/

[46] https://www.redbrand.com/deer-orchard-wildlife-fence/

[47] https://www.deerbusters.com/7-5-deer-fence-complete-kits/

[48] https://naturalresources.extension.iastate.edu/encyclopedia/white-tailed-deer-damage-management

[49] Food Scraps in your Lasagna compost: Food scraps are great to compost and it's rewarding to have your food scraps become your future food. The one caution is that your raised beds need to be in a place where you will not attract rodents or wildlife to dig them up. Some dogs will go for the smell of vegetable scraps as well. Coffee grounds and tea leaves will be OK. Never include meat or dairy.

[50] https://extension.oregonstate.edu/gardening/techniques/sheet-mulching-aka-lasagna-composting-builds-soil-saves-time

https://www.bbg.org/gardening/article/make_a_lasagna_garden_in_a_raised_bed *This article was originally published in Brooklyn Botanic Garden's handbook **Easy Compost**.*

[51] Raised-Bed Gardening for Beginners: Everything You Need to Know to Start and Sustain a Thriving Garden, Tammy Wylie. Rockridge Press, Emeryville, California, 2019.

[52] I've had one of these for more than 20 years. I love it. https://www.amazon.com/Atree-Moisture-Monitor-Humidity-Hygrometer/dp/B07WCGBQ43/ref=sr_1_4?dchild=1&keywords=moisture+thermometer+for+plants&qid=1591199165&sr=8-4

www.ingramcontent.com/pod-product-compliance
Lightning Source LLC
Chambersburg PA
CBHW050319120526
44592CB00014B/1972